Tree Model Optimized for Precisely Predicting Location-Based Services from User Behavior Data

VENKATESH M

Contents

CHAPTER 1

INTRODUCTION

1.1 INTRODUCTION

A social network is a collection of individuals connected by one or more types of relationships, such as friendship, shared knowledge, and common interest. Location data adds strength to social networks. A space can be specified as relative, absolute, and symbolic. Location is commonly referred to as three types of geographical representations–a point, a region, and a trend. In recent times, localization strategies enhance social networking services and allow users to share their location-related content, geo-tagged photos and notes. This is known as location-based social networks (LBSNs). This chapter also includes a brief review on the available techniques. Further, the discussion on various methodologies to be applied on different datasets with related existing requirements.

1.2 BACKGROUND

The task of extracting significant knowledge in the form of groups and patterns has become strenuous and necessary due to the tremendous growth in the degree and density of data. There are a lot of patterns in biology which are yet to be understood and data mining helps to ascertain unusual and hopefully useful information. Web based repositories have collected a very huge amount of data in sequence and functional genome projects

(Baldi & Brunak 2001). It is a complicated task to analyze these data manually. Therefore, sophisticated computing techniques are necessary to extract new, meaningful, and useful information from these data. In the past few years, data mining techniques have been successfully applied in such analysis.

1.2.1 Introduction to Clustering and Clustering Techniques

The advent of advanced techniques like microarray technology has led to a surge in the amount of location based data generated. As a result, there is an emerging and increasing need for technology to extract useful and rational fundamental patterns of location based information inherent in these data. Clustering technology is one of the useful and popular methods to obtain these patterns. Clustering technique, which is an essential step in data mining process, has proved to be useful in finding interesting patterns in location based data. In cluster analysis, one wishes to partition the given dataset into groups based on the given features such that the data objects in the same group are more similar to each other than the data objects in other groups. The objects are clustered or grouped based on the principle of maximizing intra-class similarity and minimizing interclass similarity.

During cluster analysis, location based data are clustered based on similarity. Proximity measurement measures the similarity (or distance) between two data objects (Halkidi *et al.* 2001).The proximity between two objects O_i and O_j is measured by a proximity function of corresponding vectors of O_i and O_j. Euclidean distance is one of the most commonly used methods to measure the distance between two data objects. It is a true metric as it satisfies the inequality triangle. The location based data matrix is to be properly normalized before using Euclidean distance. As the Euclidean distance takes the magnitude of the location data into account, it preserves many information about the data and can be preferred in certain situations. The main drawback is that Euclidean distance does not score well for scaled patterns or profiles of location based. The Manhattan distance is closely related to Euclidean distance. This finds out the sum of distances along each dimension while Euclidean distance finds the length of the shortest path between two points.

Another measure is Pearson's correlation coefficient, which measures the similarity between the shapes of two expression patterns (profiles). Pearson's correlation coefficient views each object as a random variable with k observations and calculates the linear relationship between the distribution of two random variables in order to measure the similarity between two objects. Pearson's correlation coefficient is widely used and has proved to be efficient in many clustering algorithm for location based data (Daxin *et al.* 2004, Anindya & Rajat 2009). The main drawback of this measure is that it is not more robust in handling outliers. In order to address the problems faced with Pearson's correlation coefficient, another measure named Spearsman correlation coefficient was introduced. This measure is an example of non-parametric similarity measure. It is more robust against outliers when compared to Pearson's correlation coefficient. In addition to this, other similarity measures like Squared Correlation Coefficient, Minkowski's Distance and Cosine Similarity are also available.

1.2.2 Soft Data Mining

Soft computing is an association of methodologies like fuzzy sets, neural networks, genetic algorithms that helps in flexibly handling real-life problems. Soft computing methodologies aim to exploit imprecision, uncertainty, approximate reasoning and partial truth. Data mining when integrated with soft computing techniques is regarded as 'soft data mining'. Figure 1.1 illustrates the constituents and activities under the umbrella of soft data mining. The application of soft data mining in data sets helps to uncover interesting, new patterns. The problem of imprecise knowledge has become a crucial issue for computer scientist. Though there are many approaches for handling this issue, the most admirable one is the fuzzy sets proposed by Zadeh (1965). The basic concept of this theory is possibility measures. Then Pawlak introduced rough set theory in 1980's. Similar to fuzzy sets. rough set theory is not an alternative to classical set theory but embedded in it. In Rough set theory, imprecision is expressed by a boundary region of a set, and not by a partial membership, like in fuzzy set theory.

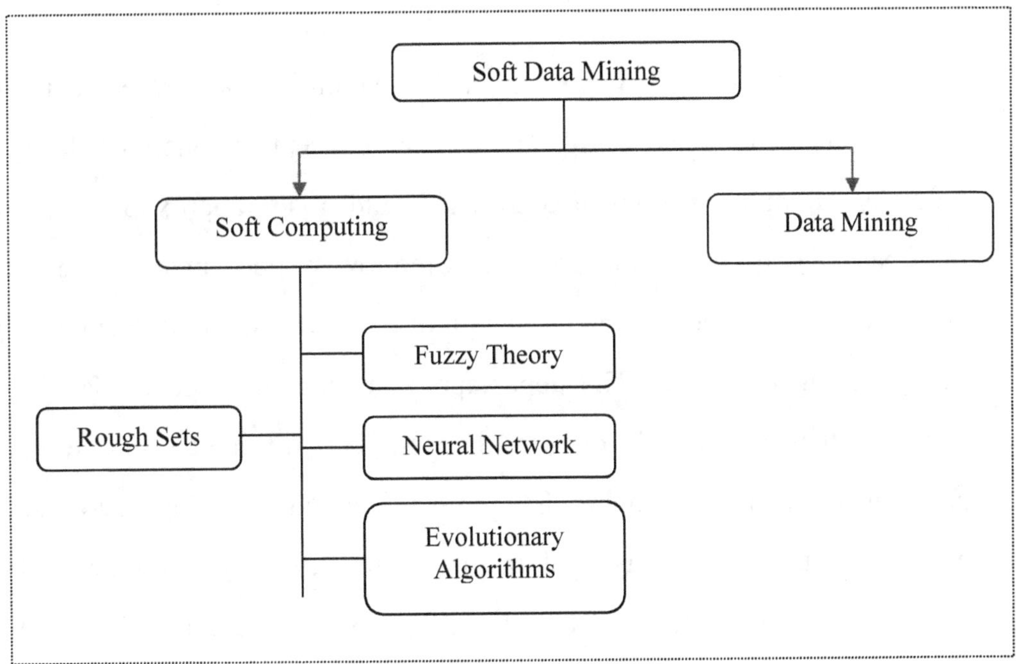

(Source: Dash & Dehuri 2012)

Figure 1.1 Constituents of Soft Data mining

Rough sets make an approximation of sets using a collection of elementary sets. Methodology based on Rough set does not require external parameters to analyze data and to draw conclusions from them. It offers many opportunities for developing Knowledge Discovery methods using partition properties and the discernibility matrix. Rough sets theory provides a mathematical tool that can be used to find out all possible feature subsets (Liu & Setiono 1996, Liu & Setiono 1997, Pawlak 1982, Pawlak *et al.* 1995). In the feature selection problem the principal idea is to recognize the dispensable and indispensable features, using the discernibility matrix (Nguyen *et al.* 1996, Pawlak *et al.* 1995). The purpose of using Rough sets is to find the Core, that is, the set of all crucial features.

1.2.3   Introduction to Rough Set Concepts

Rough set theory has attracted attention of many researchers and practitioners all over the world. The original concept of rough set theory is induction of approximations of concepts. The idea is to approximate a subset by a pair of two precise concepts called the lower approximation and upper approximation. The lower approximation of a set consists of all elements that surely belong to the set. The upper approximation of a set consists of all elements that possibly belong to the set. The difference in the upper approximation and lower approximation is the boundary region. It consists of elements that cannot be classified uniquely to the set or its compliment. Thus, Rough sets unlike crisp sets have non empty boundary region. This section defines some basic concepts related to Rough sets theory.

Definition 1. Equivalence relation

Let U be a non-empty set and let x, y, and z be elements of U. Consider R such that xRy if and only if (x,y) is in R. R is an equivalence relation if it satisfies the following proporties:

i)   Reflexive Property: (x, x) is in R for all x in U.

ii)   Symmetric Property: if (x, y) is in R, then (y, x) is in R.

iii)   Transitive Property: if (x, y) and (y, z) are in R, then (x, z) is in R.

Definition 2. Partition

A partition P of U is a family of nonempty subsets of U such that each element of U is contained in exactly one element of P as shown in Equations (1.1) and (1.2).

$$U = \bigcup_{i=1}^{n} U_i \tag{1.1}$$

$$U_i \cap U_j = \emptyset, \text{ for all } i \neq j \tag{1.2}$$

Definition 3. The Indiscernibility relation

Rough sets theory is based on the Indiscernibility relation. Let T=(U, A, C, D) be a decision system data, where U is a non-empty finite set called the universe, A is a set of features, C and D are subsets of A, named the conditional and decisional attributes subsets respectively. The elements of U are called objects, cases, instances or observations. Attributes are interpreted as features, variables or characteristics conditions. Given a feature a, such that:

$a: U \rightarrow V_a$ for a$\in$A, V_a is called the value set of a. Let a $\in$ A, P$\subseteq$ A, the indiscernibility relation Ind(P), is defined as in Equation (1.3).

$$Ind(P) = \{(x, y) \in U \times U : \forall\, a \in P, a(x) = a(y)\} \qquad (1.3)$$

In simple words, two objects are indiscernible if we cannot discern between them, because they do not differ enough. The indiscernibility relation defines a partition in U. Let U/Ind(P) denote a family of all equivalence classes of the relation Ind(P), called elementary sets. Two other equivalence classes U/Ind(C) and U/Ind(D), called conditional and decisional classes respectively, can also be defined.

The equivalence classes of the discernibility relation, which are the minimal blocks of the information system, can be used to approximate these concepts. A set X approximated using upper and lower approximation is depicted in Figure 1.2.

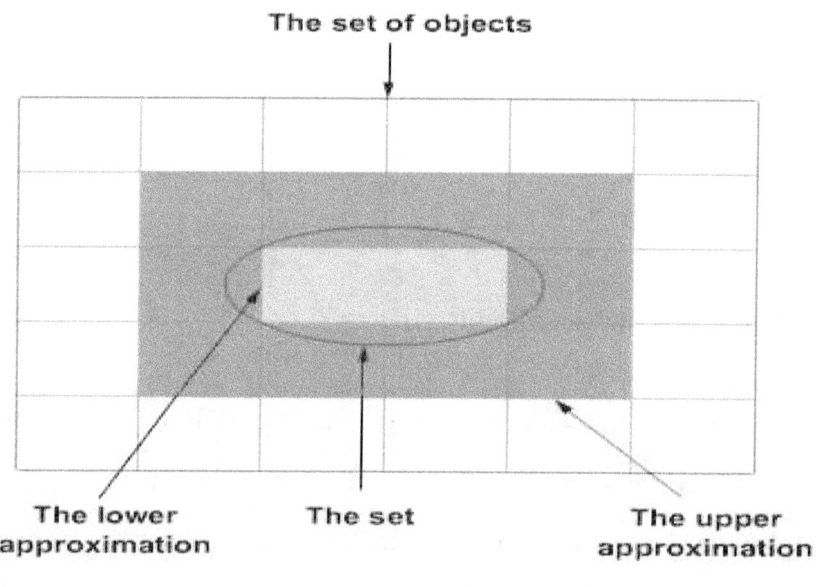

(Source: Pawlak 1982)

Figure 1.2 Representation of data partitioning for X

Definition 4. Lower approximation of a subset

Let $R \subseteq C$ and $X \subseteq U$, the R-lower approximation set of X, is the set of all elements of U which can be with certainty classified as elements of X.

$$R_*(X) = \cup \{Y \in U / R : Y \subseteq X\} \tag{1.4}$$

According to this definition and the Equation (1.4), we can see that R-Lower approximation is a subset of X, thus $R_*(X) \subseteq X$.

Definition 5. Upper approximation of a subset

The R-upper approximation set of X is the set of all element of U, that can possibly belong to the subset of interest X. The R-upper approximation can be given as in Equation (1.5).

$$R^*(X) = \cup \{Y \in U / R : Y \cap X \neq \emptyset\} \tag{1.5}$$

Note that X is a subset of the R-upper approximation set, thus $X \subseteq R^*(X)$.

Definition 6. Boundary Region.

It is the collection of elementary sets defined by Equation (1.6)

$$B(X) = R^*(X) - R_*(X) \tag{1.6}$$

These sets are included in R-Upper but not in R-Lower approximations.

Definition 7. Rough Set

A subset defined through its lower and upper approximations is called a Rough set. That is, when Equation (1.7) holds,

$$R^*(X) \neq R_*(X) \tag{1.7}$$

the boundary region is a non-empty set.

Definition 8. Crisp Set

A subset is called Crisp when its boundary region is empty as shown in Equation (1.8).

$$R^*(X) = R_*(X). \tag{1.8}$$

Definition 9. Accuracy of the approximation

The accuracy of the approximation to the set X from the elementary subsets is measured as the ratio of the lower and the upper approximation size and is given in Equation (1.9). The ratio is equal to 1, if no boundary region exists, which indicates a perfect classification. In this case, deterministic rules for the data classification can be generated.

$$a(X) = L(X)/U(X) \tag{1.9}$$

Thus, a set X with accuracy equal to 1 is crisp, otherwise X is rough.

1.2.4   Relationship between Crisp Sets, Fuzzy Sets and Rough Sets

Fuzzy sets introduced by Zadeh in 1965 and Rough sets introduced by Pawlak in 1982 are methods that can be viewed as representations of uncertainty regarding set membership. Fuzzy sets use the membership function to give a degree of membership. A fuzzy set on a classical set X is defined as in Equation (1.10).

$$\tilde{F} = \{(x, \mu_a(x)) : x \in X\} \tag{1.10}$$

$\mu_a(x)$ denotes the fuzzy membership function. A subset F is a fuzzy set when its membership in X is not crisp, but it is subject to gradation; formally this is expressed in the interval [0, 1], by the fuzzy membership function. The membership function $\mu_a(x)$ quantifies the grade of membership of the elements x to the fundamental set X. An element mapping to the value 0 means that the member is not included in the given set, 1 describes a fully included member. Values strictly between 0 and 1 characterize the fuzzy members. In Rough set theory, imprecision is expressed by a boundary region of a set, and not by a partial membership, like in fuzzy set theory.

In Rough sets the equivalence classes generate the lower and upper approximations for a subset X. Rough sets theory does not work with crisp sets. A Crisp set has a clear cut point, hence does not reflect uncertainty about membership. For this reason, Crisp sets are used to formally characterize a concept. Rough sets are used to approximate sets. The rough membership function quantifies the degree or relative overlap between the set X and the equivalence class to which the current argument belongs to.

1.3   LBSN AND EXISTING SOCIAL NETWORKS

LBSN adds a location to existing social networks and suggests that people in their social networks can share information about their location. Based on location-related information, a new abbreviation is available and the attached person is location, related content, photos, texts, and videos. The immediate location and a person's history are presented as a timestamp for a specific period. The location dimension updates the gaps between health and digital online social networking services, improving new features, challenging objects and relationships in the following aspects and challenging intellectual instruction. The user is one of the most important elements of the environment, and encompasses a detailed knowledge of the user's interests and behaviours, not only according to the user's behaviour, but also on the user's movement and his physical activities. In recent times, location based services such as tour guides and location based social networks have collected a lot of data. Today, positioning activity on mobile devices such as GPS phones helps people to easily know their locations. This location data provides various locations based services on the web and is attractive to users. In real time, data is large, but data warehouses use small-scale databases of users that are recommended. In real-time scenarios, these techniques fail because millions of users use social networks at the same time.

1.3.1   Location-based Social Networks

LBSNs are social networks, allowing users to share their locations and let others know where they are. Recognizing users who have been tagged to a location will help users to view results, such as shopping or places to eat. Popular LSPS includes Facebook Places, Google Plus, Google Latitude, Kovalla, Pride Kit, Twitter, Flickr and Foursquare, all of which share information in text, film, audio or video format. Although privacy concerns are at risk, these location-encoded data are widely used in applications. These sites, including checks and details of users in specific locations, including posts and references to others using specific locations.

Some sites offer some of the application programming interfaces (APIs) needed to access the data needed. In any case, you can allow access to and access data for more use. They can analyze it, decide on users or their personal preferences, a great way to share the time or time for users in the future, or similar users. There are additional attributes like time, cost, distance, season, climate, weather conditions, attachment between locations, and in combination with check formats, to provide better recommendations to places or users. Here, the authors already think that the places visited by users should not be brought back to their attention and should be advised to either directly or indirectly by members of the community or user community.

They already know the places visited by users, and more than 75% of them want to visit new places than those who have already visited. Many tests and inspections used data from Foursquare, Pride Kit and Gowalla. Foursquare allows users to check in specific locations and release their check-in details on Twitter or Facebook. You can download information from Twitter or Facebook or Foursquare. They will meet the authentication requirements of the sites.

1.3.2   Personality

It is debatable that personality traits are deep and natural human traits. These represent an individual's persistent state of mind, capturing how a person can approach and respond to a wide range of situations throughout their lives. Trait theorists argue that these predispositions influence behaviour, and that personality traits have been shown to influence a wide range of human activities, including consumer marketing, student behaviour, work performance, musical taste, change leadership, travel behaviour, and residential decisions.

As far as technology is concerned, the dimensions of personality are associated with many functions: computer self-efficacy, mobile phone usage, social networking activity for Twitter, online (rather than location) Facebook usage, media consumption and broader Internet activity.

Working with the types of scenarios that are consistent with individual activity personality traits illustrate aspects including: independence from the structure, lack of behavioural expectations, autonomy, self-expression, ability to engage in abilities, and support for relationships with others. It characterizes the freedom of decision-making for many everyday activities, such as consumer-related and social situations. Although there has been some debate, there has been general consensus on the use of a five-factor model that assesses personality in terms of openness, conscience, agreement, extraversion, and neuroticism.

Transparency involves attributes such as originality, curiosity, spontaneity and imagination. Open-ended higher levels may indicate an artistic character, with the desire to increase the breadth and depth of thoughts, views and experiences. Less openness may mean a more conservative or conventional approach. Conscience is associated with attributes such as organization, resourcefulness, perseverance and perseverance. A high score on conscience refers to a focused and organized approach to everyday activities. Extraversion is associated with sociality, commitment, outreach and communication with others. Those who score higher tend to be more sociable with larger groups, while those with lower scores tend to be more reserved and introverted. Agreement is associated with cooperative, courteous, and empathetic behaviours that they believe in and avoid conflict. Neuroticism is associated with impulsivity and emotional instability, and involves negative emotional expression. Neurological scores are higher in those who experience stress, anxiety, and sensitivity to threats.

Consistent with other work, we used the dimensions of the five-factor model estimated by a questionnaire to measure personality. Short tool helps in data collection when participants are not supervised, such as web-based views.

1.4 TYPES OF RECOMMENDATION SYSTEMS

Online recommendation system can be classified into personalized and non-personalized methods. The non-personalized methods do not consider the characteristics and preference of the online user; whereas personalized method tightly depends on the user profile. Non personalized method does not require much calculation. It uses simple statistical analysis to make recommendations. The user profile personalized method can be further classified to persistent and ephemeral personalization based on whether life time of background information used for the recommendation is either persistent or transient. In persistent method, there are 2 types of filtering methods viz. demographic and collaborative. The content filtering is an ephemeral personalization method. In demographic based filtering, it uses the demographic (Kruwlich 1997) information about users to make recommendations. In collaborative filtering method (Burke 2002), system identifies the past web navigation of user whose tastes are similar to current user navigations and recommends the social networks what they have linked. But, this method is challenged with cold start problem.

This problem arises when the system encounters the user with new navigations that have not been recorded in the background data. Thus, collaborative filtering method is not efficient due to cold start problem. This method is effective only if it has enough background data. In content based filtering (Kadushin *et al.* 2004) method, social network is recommended to user based on the past accessed social network link content. The main limitation of the method is overlapping of content recommendation and thus the customer may be bored by the continuous watching of the overlapping content. Recently, hybrid approach is proposed in online recommendation system which combines both the content and collaborative based filtering. This approach eliminates the drawbacks of each of these methods and takes the full advantage of both methods. Both these method complement each other and contribute to each other's success.

The major challenges to be addressed in the LBSN recommendation are 1) location-context awareness; 2) heterogeneous domains and 3) rate of development. The recommendation system for LBSNs uses a variety of data sources, including 1) user profiles, 2) user online history, and 3) user location history. This real-time display includes large amounts of data. Most systems in LBSNS use only one type of data source to make a system recommendation. In addition, many data sources are related and mutual robustness. Furthermore, considering various data sources, you can provide the most useful suggestions. For example, the user's online interaction, social structure, and location history are compatible with all friend recommendations. If two users have more online connections, they are closer to the social structure and linked to the location history, and these users may be compatible. A friend recommendation system that can consider all of these factors will make high quality friend recommendations.

1.4.1   Content-based Recommendation Systems

The content-based inspector provides the user with an explicit (rating) or implicit (clicking link). Based on that data, a user profile is created, which is used to make recommendations to the user. The user provides additional entries or takes action on recommendations; The machine will become more accurate. Time flag (TF) and inverse document frequency (IDF) observations are used in information-receiving systems and material-based filtration mechanisms (such as content-based analyzers). They are used to ascertain the reliability of a document / article / news item / film.

On this system, keywords are used to describe the items, and the user is designed to specify the item types that the user wants. In other words, these protocols have tried to recommend a user that the user liked in the past or is currently considering. It does not really rely on the user login program to create a temporary profile. In particular, various candidate items are better suited to the user than previously rated items. This approach has its roots in information retrieval and information filtering research.

Basically, these methods use the profile of an item (i.e. a set of distinct features and attributes) that represents the item in the system. The item supply algorithm will be used to ignore features on the system. The widely used algorithm is the word frequency and inverse document frequency (tf-idf) representation (also known as vector space representation). The system creates a content-based profile of users based on a weighted vector of item items. The load indicates the importance of each aspect, and is calculated in vectors with different rated materials using a variety of techniques. While the simple approach, while using vector values of the rated item, other sophisticated methods use mechanical learning techniques such as Bayesian classics, cluster analysis, knot trees, and artificial neural networks to assess the user's desire for the desired item. Huh.

An important issue with content-based filtering is whether the user can know the user's choices from the user's actions and whether it can be used for the content source and other content types. When recommending the same type of content that a user already uses, the value of the system will be lower when it provides other content types from other services. For example, it is useful to suggest news articles based on browsing messages, but are very useful when different services are recommended based on browsing news such as music, videos, products, discussions, etc. Use some hybridsystems.

Content-based recommendations may also include response-based recommendations. In some cases, users are allowed to leave a text review or response. These user-generated texts contain clear data on recommendation as they are an efficient source of features / features and ratings / consciousness of users. Features extracted from user-generated reviews improve meta-data because they reflect features of objects such as meta-data, and features extracted are widely concerned about users. Special features extracted from ratings are considered users' ratings in relevant aspects. Popular approaches to response-based recommendations use several techniques; including intelligence, information retrieval, and emotional analysis.

1.4.2   Collaborative Filtering-based Recommendation Systems

One approach to the design of systems recommended for universal use is a composite filter. Based on the assumption, in which people in the past agreed on the future and based on the idea that they would like the same things in the past as they would like. The system makes recommendations using information about aggregate profiles for different users or objects. If the peer user / item has a rating history like the current user or item, they can make recommendations using this neighborhood. User and item-based close neighbor algorithms can cope with the cold start problem and improve the recommendation results using this data. Combination filtering methods can be memory based and modeling based. A well-known example of a memory-based approach is user-based instruction, while model-based approaches are kernel-mapping recommendations.

An important advantage of the integrated filtering approach is that it does not rely on machine analysis materials, so the item has the ability to accurately suggest complex things such as films without 'understanding'. Several methods are used to measure item recognition in user unity or system systems.

1.4.3   Link Analysis-based Recommendation Systems

It is assumed that the referral system will work on an interconnected network consisting of nodes and connecting links. The method is commonly used in the context of location or user recommendation to identify experienced users and popular locations. Link analysis methods are used for this purpose, the most commonly used methods are hypertext-induced Topic search (HITS) and PageRank.

Here the Users are related to experience score and popularity. If more users visit a location, its popularity score increases and if a user visits more locations, his experience score increases. This score can then be used to determine popular locations and experienced users (Zheng *et al.* 2009).

1.4.4   Knowledge-based Recommendation Systems

This type of Knowledge-based systems require user knowledge and domain knowledge. Case-based recommendations and control-based recommendations are the two main methods used in Knowledge based recommendation systems. Case-based recommendations require explicit domain knowledge, while control-based recommendations rely on explicit restrictions or filters in the domain. There may be interactive conversations between the user and the system, asking about the needs of the system's users, either by answering questions or answering them via SMS. (Burke 2002).

1.4.5   Hybrid Recommendation Systems

Most recommended systems now combine mixed filtering, content-based filtering and other approaches and use a hybrid approach. There is no reason why many of the same varieties are not hybrid. Hybrid policies can be implemented in several ways: by integrating them separately and then through content-based and collaborative-based calculations; By adding (and vice versa) content-specific skills to a collaborative-oriented approach; Or by integrating the sampling process. Numerous studies comparing hybrids with complete hybrid and content-based methods provide evidence that hybrid methods can provide more accurate recommendations than complete approaches. These techniques serve to address some of the common problems of recommendation systems, such as cold weather and minor problems, as well as the engineering problem of science in a knowledge-based approach. Netflix is a good example of the use of hybrid recommendation systems.

1.5 APPLICATIONS OF RECOMMENDATION SYSTEMS

Applications for recommendations are broadly available with key applications including products, movies, music, services, users, activities, events and places. Most of the cases, these applications are customer or user satisfied. Users' preference should be successfully taken into account. Netflix, Movie Lens and Amazon Web Systems are some of the examples of recommendation systems.

1.6 MOTIVATION

Recently, a number of studies have been proposed to develop a more accurate online recommendation system which has the capability to capture the future navigation pattern of online users. An extensive survey of the online recommendation system and architecture used in the commercial and academic research with respect to the proposed system is made. Dayal *et al.* (1996) proposed a system called Analog which is one of the first WUM based online recommendation system. It consist of online and offline component. The offline component builds session clusters by analyzing user navigation pattern recorded in the log file. In the online component part, active user session is classified according to the generated model. This classification identifies the pages that match with the active session and returns the requested page with list of suggestions. Clustering approach of system is challenged by several limitations especially with scalability and accuracy. There are varieties of clustering algorithms available for usage. Each approach could have different type of clusters [Exclusive (K-Means), Overlapping (Fuzzy C Means) and Hierarchical]. It's difficult to compare the performance of algorithm on large dataset like web log. In addition, clustering approach used in all recommendation systems needs to be backed up by good classification method. Analog system does not have the proper classification approach over the overlapping cluster.

Today's attention has turned to location, travel, activity and user recommendations. The travelers around the world have been using these systems deliberately introducing their travel plans, as they serve as a reliable and neutral source for real advice during the journey. Provide timely recommendations for response requests. Map Reduce paradigm could be utilized to exploit parallelism. So, the researchers were encouraged to pursue research.

1.7   PROBLEM STATEMENT

User activity is predicted through the frequency in which the online substances in location-based social networks (LBSN) are produced and used by the consumer. Users are classified by researchers into a number of groups depending upon the level of their functioning. This work involves gradient boosted distributed decision tree (GBDT) which is optimised on the basis of total iterations and shrinkage on using best algorithm. Implementation of the data is done through Hadoop network. A foursquare dataset is created using work, food, travel, park and shop. One of the most commonly used machine learning algorithm is stochastic gradient boosted decision trees (GBDT) at present. The node with lowest lower bound is developed through best first search (BFS). Its own filing system is provided through Hadoop which is called Hadoop distributed file system (HDFS). The algorithm used is K-nearest Neighbour (KNN) classifier algorithm. The proposed online recommendation system is a hybrid approach which implements both the collaborative and content based filtering methods.

1.8 ORGANIZATION OF THESIS

There are six chapters in this thesis.

Chapter 1 deals with the introduction to the organization of mining location-based online services, motivation and thesis.

Chapter 2 describes in detail the literature survey conducted in the areas of quantitative analysis of the location-based online services mining and other interruption decision tree method.

Chapter 3 discusses and deals with the training of existing systems. The discussion focuses on the terminology of various existing algorithms.

Chapter 4 discusses and deals with the training of the proposed system. The discussion focuses on the new Best First Gradient Destination Decision Tree method architecture and terminology of various training algorithms.

Chapter 5 focuses on the topmost and bottommost results, calculating degree evaluation values and mining measures. Performance measures of various methods are also discussed.

Chapter 6 discusses the completion and future scope of the work.

1.9   SUMMARY

The suggested systems from research pioneers have proven to be hot and trendy sites. There are various referral systems, such as location and travel referrer systems that are priceless for these days due to their need and use. It is clear that especially in case of environmental awareness; it is possible to prevent problems in handling of location and travel recommendations. The lack of features or their deterioration in the current system must be clearly addressed in the proposed manner.

CHAPTER 2

LITERATURE REVIEW

2.1   INTRODUCTION

Recommendation System is a data mining technique that has been widely used on location based data. A lot of research work has been done on this topic and new methods for analyzing location based data keep evolving. This chapter provides an overview of the research carried out on Recommendation System algorithms and their applications to several microarray data reported in literature. A detailed study has been done on the advantages of various recommender system and drawbacks of existing system used in our day-to-day life. The study reveals that there is a race for an architecture/framework which reduces the complexity especially like large data volume reality system where small scale datasets are provided but the data volume is huge.

A review of the various techniques adopted in the current work on recommendation methods is presented in detail in this chapter. Different recommendation systems - content-based, collaborative filtering-based, hybrid recommendation and their types - are provided. Furthermore, the shortcomings of the existing systems are examined and presented, followed by the contributions of the proposed work.

2.2   LITERATURE SURVEY

A significant role is played by recommender system in our day-to-day life. Online recommendation system called SUGGEST (Baraglia *et al.* 2005) which provides useful information in optimizing web server performance which made navigation easier for the web user. SUGGEST adopts a two level architecture composed of offline creation of historical knowledge and online component that understands the user's behaviour. SUGGEST uses the markov model (Deshpande *et al.* 2004) for calculating the probability of a page the web user visit in future after visiting pages in the same session. This system uses the markov model to improve the accuracy. The limitation of the system is not suitable for the web site made up of dynamically generated pages. Similarly, Mobasher *et al.* (2003) proposed a Web Personalizer system which provides dynamic recommendation, as a list of hyperlinks to users. Web Personalizer system analysis is based on the usage data combined with structure formed by the hyperlinks of site. Aggregated usage profile is obtained by applying data mining technology i.e clustering and association rule after the preprocessing phase. In data mining phase, web server logs are converted into clusters made up of set of pages with the common usage characteristics.

The online phase considers the active user session in order to find match among the user activities and discover usage profile. Matching entries are then used to compute a set of recommendations which will be inserted into the last requested page as a list of hypertext links. However, the accuracy of the Web Personalizer is affected by association rule mining which is used for the discovery of frequent item sets in web log data. The main problem with the association rule mining method is discovery of contradictory association rules that degrades the prediction accuracy. Middleton *et al.* (2004) proposed a hybrid approach which combines the collaborative and content based filtering methods. This method is implemented in the academic research article website where a scholar get the recommendation links to research article based on their current visit and their research profile. All the user profiles are characterized using the ontological concept. Even though the system characterizes the each user profile as ontological concept, it doesn't have the component to track the changing needs of the users. Etminani *et al.* (2009) proposed the SOM based web usage mining method to discover the user's navigational patterns from server log files. However, this method has not given importance to capture the current interest of online user.

Xiaozhe Wang *et al.* (2005) proposed the Soft Computing Paradigms (SCP) based on WUM method to discover usage patterns from the available statistical data obtained from the Web server log files. In their work, data clustering is performed using Self Organizing Map and the clustered data are fed to three popular SCP including Takagi Sugeno Fuzzy Inference System (TSFIS), Artificial Neural Networks (ANNs) and Linear Genetic Programming (LGP). This SCP based model is developed to forecast the access pattern of web user. However, this model has not given the importance to web personalization but it focuses on the web traffic analysis. Similarly, Most of the research efforts related to the online recommendation system discussed above depend heavily on the website usage data which is available in the form of log file. Most of the existing online recommendation systems like Analog, Web Personalizer, and Suggest often make the wrong prediction and false recommendation to the users at uncertainty situation that arise when system classifies the current user navigation to overlapping navigation profile. Also, the most valuable information like semantic relationship between the web pages of the site and the changing needs of the user over a period of time is not considered in these systems. Therefore, the accuracy of these related systems is not up to the expectation. An item which interests a user is suggested automatically by a recommender system. Recommendations based on locations are provided by small-scale datasets but in reality the data volume is huge. The necessity for big data is studied through foursquare dataset for big data in systems recommended for LBSN. Only some quality criteria such as parallel processing and multimodal interface have been chosen to learn necessitate for big data in recommender systems. Narayanan & Cherukuri (2016) made a learning and investigation of eminence parameters of recommendation systems for LBSN with big data. Everyone would have enjoyed the recommendation system on the web. When we sign in to Youtube, we automatically get a list of recommended videos. When we log on to Amazon or Flipkart, we are given a list of recommended products. Facebook provides us with a list of friend suggestions. When we search on Google, it throws out the recommended search text. These are all different kinds of suggestions. The success of these types of referral sites depends on the amount and quality of available data. These days, data availability is not a problem, thanks to big data and Hadoop. Recommended machines are one of the easiest parts to get started when dealing with machine learning.

Recommendation System is mostly one of the first steps in location based analysis. Variety of Recommendation System algorithms has been proposed for Recommendation System location based data. Many extensive reviews on the Recommendation System algorithm when applied on location based data are available. Kerr *et al.* (2007) have done a study on all state of art techniques which recognizes their drawbacks and addresses them. Daxin *et al.* (2004) have done a brief review of the recommendation system algorithms and have categorized them into four main groups namely, content-based recommendations, collaborative recommendations, utility based recommendations and hybrid approaches. Patrick (2005) has clearly pictured how location based recommendation System works, what to expect out of it and what not to and how to evaluate the recommendation system algorithms. Gengxin *et al.* (2002) have evaluated and compared few recommendation system algorithms which helps us to select a suitable recommendation system algorithm. Others like Sharon *et al.* (2002), Michiel *et al.* 2002) have also done an analysis on different recommendation system algorithm and their applications to location based data.

A detailed survey, study and analysis of the algorithms have also been done as part of this research work and presented here. Recommendation system algorithms can be classified based on the structure of the data generated, whether it yields partial or complete data, or whether it is exclusive or overlapping. Though there are different ways in which recommendation system algorithms can be categorized, it is presented here, categorized as partition based algorithms, Hierarchical based algorithms, density based algorithms, model based methods, pattern based algorithms and so on. Priyanka Das et al. (2019) proposed group incremental clustering algorithm is adapted to provide the updated set of clusters. The method has been applied on various crime report datasets and validated with the help of several cluster validation indices. The method is also compared with some state-of-the-art clustering algorithms to express its effectiveness and statistical significance in the domain of crime corpora.

2.3   CONTENT BASED RECOMMENDATION SYSTEM METHODS

The most popular class of recommendation system algorithms is the combinatorial optimization algorithms also referred to as iterative relocation algorithms. These algorithms minimize a given recommendation system criterion by iteratively relocating data points between data until an optimal partition is attained. Content-based Recommendation System attempts to directly decompose the data set into a set of disjoint data. In a basic iterative algorithm, such as K-means or K-medoids, convergence is local and the globally optimal solution cannot be guaranteed. Content based algorithm tend to create data that are spherical in shape as they are distance based.

The k-means algorithm (McQueen 1967), the most widely known, is a typical partition based algorithm. The k-means recommendation system algorithm has four steps: initialization, assigning, calculation and iteration. Given a prespecified number K, the algorithm partitions the data set into K disjoint subsets. Initially the algorithm starts with a randomly initialized cluster centers. The objects that are closer to the center are grouped together to form a cluster. With the objects assigned to the data, new cluster centers are formed. This procedure iterates until there is no change in the cluster centers. The data are formed based on an objective function that minimizes the distance between the object and the cluster center. The distance is measured using Euclidean distance. The Euclidean distance between objects (gi,gj) can be given as in Equation (2.1).

$$d(gi, gj) = \sqrt{\sum_k (x_{ik} - x_{jk})^2} \tag{2.1}$$

This algorithm is simple and fast. An Analysis on this algorithm shows that K-means algorithm converges after a few iterations.

Several variations of K-means algorithms have been applied to location based data. K means+ method (Heng *et al.* 2005) addresses the number of data dependency and degeneracy. K-means+ method can automatically partition the location based data into a reasonable number of data and then the informative location data are selected from data. An enhanced K-means recommendation system algorithm (Jirong *et al.* 2009) has been proposed for refining initial points and it is capable of reducing execution time. This algorithm improves solutions for large data by refining the initial conditions. This refinement of initial points in the K-means algorithm greatly improves the efficiency of k-means algorithm.

The global k-means recommendation system algorithm proposed by Aristidis *et al.* (2003), presented a deterministic global optimization method that does not rely on any initial parameter values but uses the k-means algorithm as a local search procedure. Instead of arbitrarily selecting initial values for all cluster centers, this technique optimally adds one new cluster center at each stage in an incremental way. Adil & Karim (2006) developed a new or a modified version of the global k-means algorithm. This algorithm computes data incrementally and to compute k-partition of a data set it uses $k - 1$ cluster centers from the previous iteration. An important step in this algorithm is the computation of a starting point for the k-th cluster center. This starting point is computed by minimizing so-called auxiliary cluster function. The proposed algorithm computes as many data as a data set contains with respect to a given tolerance.

An Efficient Unified K-Means Recommendation System Technique (Valarmathie *et al.* 2011) is also an enhancement of k-mean algorithm were the initial number of data is determined using Expectation Maximization (EM) algorithm, a model based methodology. This approach decides the number of data by minimizing the squared error function and maximizing the correctness ratio value. Pavan *et al.* (2010) have proposed a SPSS (Single Pass Seed Selection) algorithm which is an extension of K-means++ which works well with high dimensional data sets.

Hemalatha & Vivekanandan (2008) have proposed an enhanced version of k-means Recommendation System algorithm which is claimed to be parallel and distributed. Garg & Jain (2006) have done a comparison on some of the existing variations of k-mean algorithms. They have used the synthetic sets of high dimensional data as benchmark for evaluating the algorithms and have also proposed some criteria for comparison of these recommendation system algorithms.

A comparative analysis of k-mean based algorithm namely global k-means, efficient k-means, k-means++ and x-means was done by Parvesh & Krishan (2010). The analysis shows that performance of these algorithms can be improved further with the help of fuzzy logic and rough set theory to yield better quality of data.

2.4   COLLABORATIVE RECOMMENDATION SYSTEM METHODS

Unlike content-based recommendation System, this type of recommendation system generates a hierarchical series of nested data which can be graphically represented by a tree, called dendrogram. The branches of a dendrogram denote the formation of data by indicating the similarity between the data. The levels in the dendogram also mark the number of data obtained. Similar objects are placed together by reordering the objects such that the branches of the corresponding dendrogram do not cross. Collaborative recommendation system algorithms can be further separated into agglomerative approaches and divisive approaches based on how the hierarchical dendrogram is constructed. Agglomerative algorithms follow a bottom-up approach. Initially each data object is considered as an individual cluster, and at each step, the closest pair of data are merged together until all the groups are merged into one cluster. Divisive algorithms follow top-down approach. It starts with a single cluster containing all the data objects and, at each step split, until single data of individual objects are formed.

Bernard *et al.* (2010) have proposed a novel hybrid approach that combines the merits of hierarchical and k-means recommendation system. This approach is different from other methods as it initially carries out collaborative recommendation system to decide location and number of data and then run the K-means Recommendation System as the next step. This approach also provides a mechanism to handle outliers.

Ranjan & Khalil (2007) have worked with the statistical approaches in this type of recommendation system and have also done a comparison on the linkage methods which can assist us in knowing the functionalities of many location based data like information about a town or city. Vijendra (2011) has presented a detailed review of various subspace and collaborative recommendation system algorithms, their efficiencies and inefficiencies on different data sets. Zhou *et al.* (2007) have proposed a Join-Prune algorithm that shows momentous gain in runtime and quality.

Nurul *et al.* (2009) have introduced a robust recommendation System algorithm for location based data analysis. This algorithm proves to provide improved performance than the traditional hierarchical algorithm in the presence of outliers.

A new collaborative recommendation system algorithm which reduces susceptibility to noise was proposed by Ziv *et al.* (2002). This algorithm allows a maximum of k siblings to be related directly and produces a single optimal order tree as resulting tree. A k-ary tree is efficiently constructed, where each node can have up to k children. An optimal ordering of the leaves is done and k data are combined at each step. The algorithm proves to be more robust against noise and missing values.

An enhanced collaborative recommendation system algorithm designed by Geetha *et al.* (2010) reduces the time taken to analyze large datasets. The method scans the dataset and calculates distance matrix only once and the result of recommendation system is represented as a binary tree. The algorithm finds the number of data with the help of cut distance and measures the quality with validation index in order to obtain high quality data.

2.5 UTILITY BASED RECOMMENDATION SYSTEM METHODS

Utility based recommendation system algorithms are appropriate when the data have irregular shapes. The method works by putting points together in high density areas as members of the same cluster and treating low density areas as boundaries separating two data. There are two approaches commonly used to identify high and low density areas. One approach is to define a neighborhood with a small radius around each data point and the minimum number of objects to be placed in that area for being considered as high density area. The points at the edges of the cluster are put to a density test and if they are found to be in the high density area, the cluster grows. The second approach is to define an influence function to each point. The total influence at any point is the sum of the influences from all the points. The influence will be high from nearby points and low from far away points. A threshold value should be defined to separate high influence areas from low influence areas.

Daxin *et al.* (2003) have dealt with the problem of effectively recommendation system time series location based data by introducing an algorithm, a utility-based recommendation system method. The utility-based approach has been used to produce data of high quality and robustness. The algorithm adopts the structure of hierarchical recommendation system and the mining result is in the form of two trees namely density tree and attraction tree. The attraction tree is an intermediate result that helps in the further investigation of the inner-structures, the borders and the outliers of the data. The density tree is the final result and it uncovers the hidden data in a data set.

Rosy *et al.* (2009) presents an incremental recommendation system algorithm based on a utility-based algorithm. The method was experimented with real-life datasets and compared with some well-known recommendation system algorithms in terms of z-score cluster validity measure. Seokkyung *et al.* (2004) have presented a novel utility based recommendation system algorithm, which utilizes a neighborhood defined by k-nearest neighbors. The recommendation system algorithm was developed based on KNN density estimation. For an efficient k-nearest neighbor search, different dimensionality reduction methods that are relevant for location based data were explored.

Sauravjyoti & Dhruba (2010) have suggested a recommendation system technique for location based data which is capable of handling incremental data. It is designed based on density based approach and it uses no proximity and therefore avoids the restrictions placed by them. The main advantage is that it retains the regulation information and is able to handle datasets updated incrementally.

2.6 HYBRID APPROACHES

The model based methods hypothesize a model for each of the data and find the best fit of the data to that model. Typical model based methods involve statistical approaches, probability models or neural network approaches.

Kohonen neural network, also called as self organizing maps (SOMs) is a two layer architecture for unsupervised recommendation system that was proposed by Kohonen(1982). Amel *et al.* (2008) have proposed a multi SOM recommendation system technique that overcomes the problem of the estimation of cluster numbers. The difficulty to find clear boundaries by SOM is overcome by combining SOM with k-means. Dali *et al.* (2002) applied a novel model of SOM, called double self-organizing map (DSOM) to location based data. DSOM finds the appropriate number of data clearly and visually depicts the appropriate number of data. A novel validation technique, known as figure of merit (FOM) has been employed to validate the data.

Xiang *et al.* (2004) have proposed a hybrid recommendation system approach based on Self- Organizing Maps and Particle Swarm Optimization. The algorithm improves the rate of convergence by adding a conscience factor to the Self-Organizing Maps algorithm and attempts to generate a more compact recommendation system result than SOM.

A model-based recommendation system method for time-course location based data was presented by Fang-Xiang (2004). This method uses Markov Chain Models (MCMs) to account for the inherent dynamics of time-course location based patterns. An assumption that expression patterns in the same location were generated by the same MCM is made by the algorithm. For the given number of data, the presented method computes location models using an EM algorithm and an assignment of location data to these models is done by maximizing their posterior probabilities. The qualities of the data are evaluated by using the Average Adjusted Rand Index (AARI).

2.7   ALGORITHM DESCRIPTION

To address the scalable concerns of user-based recommendation systems, item-based recommendation techniques (also called model-based) have been developed. These approaches analyze the user-item matrix to identify the relationships between different items and then use these relationships to compute a list of top-down suggestions. The main motivation behind it

These schemes mean that a customer will buy products that are similar or related to the products he / she has already purchased. Because these programs do not need to identify a similar customer environment when a referral is requested, they can lead to faster referral machines. Various schemes have been proposed to calculate the relationships between different items based on probabilistic approaches or traditional item-to-item correlations. We will explore different aspects of this method and their impact on the accuracy and efficiency of the algorithm.

## 2.8	VALIDATION TECHNIQUES

In the previous sections, a review of variety of recommendation system algorithms was presented. Recommendation system of location based data results in groups of co-expressed location, groups of samples with common characteristics, or 'blocks' of data and samples involved in specific location based processes. Though Cluster analysis acts as a tool to speed up and automate data processing, most of the cluster analysis carried out on genomic data is quite far from this end. This is mainly due to the properties like containing many more variables than samples, has high levels of noise and may have multiple missing values. These properties cause troubles to many traditional recommendation system methods and make cluster validation very essential. Another interesting part of this is that different recommendation system algorithms, or even the same recommendation system algorithm when using different parameters, generally result in completely different sets of data. Therefore, it is very important to compare various recommendation system results and select the one that best fits the true data distribution. Cluster validation is the process of assessing the quality and reliability of the cluster sets derived from various recommendation system techniques. The quality of a cluster as specified by Daxin *et al.* (2004) is mainly defined based on the similarity of the objects within a cluster (homogeneity) and the dissimilarity between two different data (separation).

Halkidi *et al.* (2001) have addressed an important issue in the recommendation system process which is about the quality assessment of the recommendation system results. The quality assessment of a cluster is vital as it relates to the natural features of the data set under concern. A review of available recommendation system validity measures and approaches has been presented.

Many different indices of cluster validity have been proposed, such as the Bezdek's partition coefficient, the Dunn's separation index, the Xie-Beni's separation index, Silhouette index, Davies-Bouldin's index, and the Gath-Geva's index, etc. A detailed analysis of the indices is not within the scope of this research work. A few of them are listed here.

The Silhouette index S_j, which characterizes the heterogeneity and isolation properties of a given cluster, X_j ($j = 1,..., c$), is given as in Equation (2.2).

$$S_j = \frac{1}{m}\sum_{i=1}^{m} s(i) \tag{2.2}$$

where m is number of samples in S_j. The Silhouette width s(i) for the ith sample in cluster Xj is defined as in Equation (2.3).

$$s(i) = b(i) - a(i)/\max\{a(i), b(i)\} \tag{2.3}$$

where a(i) is the average distance between the ith sample and all of the samples included in Xj ; 'max' is the maximum operator, and b(i) is the minimum average distance between the ith sample and all of the samples clustered in X_k ($k = 1,..., c$; $k \neq j$).

The Dunn index identifies sets of data that are compact and well separated. For any partition $U \leftrightarrow X: X1 \cup X2 \cup \quad Xi \cup \quad Xb$ where Xi represents the ith cluster of such partition, the Dunn index, D, is defined as in Equation (2.4).

$$D(U) = \min_{1 \leq i \leq b} \{ \min_{\substack{i \leq j \leq b \\ j \neq i}} \{ \frac{\delta(X_i, X_j)}{\max_{1 \leq k \leq b} \{\Delta(X_k)\}} \} \}$$
(2.4)

where (Xi, Xj) defines the distance between data Xi and Xj; Δ (Xk) represents the intracluster distance of cluster X_k, and b is the number of data of partition U.

The Davies-Bouldin index aims at identifying sets of data that are compact and well separated. The Davies-Bouldin validation index, DB, is defined as in Equation (2.5).

$$DB(U) = \frac{1}{b} \sum_{i=1}^{b} \max_{i \neq j} \{ \frac{\Delta(X_i) + \Delta(X_j)}{\delta(X_i, X_j)} \}$$
(2.5)

where U, $\delta(X_i, X_j)$, $\Delta(X_i)$, $\Delta(X_j)$ and b are defined as in Equation (2.5). Small values of DB correspond to data that are compact, and whose centres are far away from each other. Therefore, the cluster configuration that minimizes DB is taken as the optimal number of data, b.

Xu *et al.* (2012) proposed a graph-based implementation of K-algorithms. Although the system deals with text clustering, the basic concept can be applied to the design of the proposed system. Lee *et al.* (2011) proposed a graph-based implementation of a large, scalable social data analysis system that only deals with textual data.

He *et al.* (2011) proposed a graph and density-based clustering algorithm. The system provides insights into the parallel programming implementation of the clustering algorithm. A detailed review of the Hadoop distributed file system is provided by Swachko *et al.* (2010).

2.9   GAP IDENTIFICATION

The prediction of where the user should visit was examined by examining the predictive power provided by various aspects of user behavior. Approximately 35 million check-ins were made by 1 million Foursquare users in more than 5 million locations across the globe, analyzed over a five-month period. A set of features aimed at controlling users' movements is proposed. Information is exploited by features such as the transition between different types of space, movement between locations, and spatial temporal features of the user's registration forms. All individual attributes based on linear regression and M5 model trees were combined into two supervised learning models, resulting in overall higher prediction accuracy. It has been found that the highest predicted accuracy is provided by the supervised method based on a combination of several features: M5 model trees can be ranked in the top 50, a prediction list. Park has proposed a new effective method for practicing K-NN query, called Pattern-Based K-NN (PP-KNN). Patterns of distant relationships are used in the proposed method among the cells in the grid code. The basic plan is to standardize long-distance relationships into concrete forms. With the help of this concept, PB-kNN significantly increases the overall efficiency of query processing. Many experiments have revealed that this technique performs current methods in terms of query processing time and storage overhead.

Zhang *et al.* (2006) combine two techniques, such as local mean-based clustering (LMC) and local scatter representation-based classification (SRC) (LWSRC), with two-stage local similarity-based classification learning (LSCL) suggested techniques. The results show that the proposed technique is more accurate, less time-consuming and explicitly explained.

Chen *et al.* (2010) derive a new methodology that includes feature fusion and multi-dictionary education. The integration of the compression sensing model was done with feature extraction to create a two-stage system. Feature fusion is used for the dictionary training process to complete a robust model.

Bakshi *et al.* (2007) showed that the magnitude of the large capillary portion captured on the front camera of a mobile device takes less time for feature extraction and matching. A phase radical localized form (PILP) is named Reduced PILP (R-PILP), which produces an applicable time speed of 1.56 times, while the vector is reduced by 20% with less damage to the verification accuracy.

Zhang *et al.* (2009) suggested a plant diseased leaf segment based on the Internet of Things (IoT). Proposed a combination of super pixel clustering, K-mean clustering, and pyramid of histograms of orientation gradients (PHOG) algorithms. The results show that the proposed technique provides a potential outcome for plant diseased leaf image segmentation and plant disease recognition.

Wang *et al.* (2010) presented an innovative visual salinity guided complex image retrieval method. The complete salt map is made by combining the direction, intensity, and color of the salt map in the Itchy visual salinity mode. The multi-facet fusion paradigm of images is approached to define the image shape more clearly.

Yu-Ting Webb *et al.* (2005) proposed a framework for spatial-temporal social and social spheres to identify users with greater influence on individuals (i.e. professionals, friends, and travel professionals). This framework can filter influential users for given conditions based on POI categories, travel distance and arrival time.

2.10   MAP REDUCE AND HADOOP

Hadoop is an open source distributed processing framework that manages data processing and storage for large data applications in a scalable cluster of computer servers. It is at the center of the ecosystem of big data technologies used primarily to support advanced analytics efforts, including predictive analytics, data mining and machine learning. Hadoop systems can handle a wide variety of structured and unstructured data, giving users more flexibility to collect process and analyze data and provide data warehouses than related databases. Hadoop was developed by computer scientists Doug Cutting and Mike Caffarella, initially supporting the implementation of Nutchh Open Source Search Engine and Web Crawler. After Google released technical documents describing its Google file system and Hadoop Map Reduce programming framework in 2003 and 2004, Cutting and Cafarella modeled previous technology plans and created a Java-based Map Reduce implementations and file sytem designed on Google's. In early 2006, when the elements separated from Nach and became a separate Apache sub-project, Cutting named Hadoop after his son's stuffed elephant. At the same time, Cutting was hired by internet service company Yahoo, which later became Hadoop's first product user in 2006. The framework evolved over the next few years, and three independent Hadoop vendors were established: Cloud Terra in 2008, MapR Technologies a year later, and Hortonworks in 2011 with a Yahoo spinoff. In addition, AWS introduced the Hadoop Cloud Service, a rebranding map, in 2009. This was before the release of Apache Hadoop 1.0.0, which was available in December 2011 after a siccesson of 0.x releases.

Hadoop's ability to process and store different types of data is especially good for big data environments. They typically contain not only large amounts of data, but also a combination of structured transaction data and Internet click stream logs, web server and mobile app logs, social media posts, customer emails, and semi-structured and unstructured information. Sensor Data Matters (IoT) from the Internet.

Formally known as Apache Hadoop, the technology was developed as part of an open source project within the Apache Software Foundation. Many vendors offer commercial Hadoop distribution, however due to the crowded market, competitive pressures have reduced the number of Hadoop vendors and then the rise of big data systems in the cloud. Switching to the cloud allows the user to store data on low-cost cloud object storage services instead of Hadoop's Nemac file system; As a result, Hadoop's role in some big data structures is reduced.

The main components of Hadoop's first iteration are MapReduce, HDFS and Hadoop Common, a collection of shared applications and libraries.

As pointed out by its name, MapReduce uses map and functions to divide processing tasks into multiple tasks running on cluster nodes where data is stored, and then connecting that result to what functions are created in a coherent package. MapReduce initially worked with both Hadoop's processing engine and Cluster Resource Manager, which directly integrated HDFS and enabled limited users to run MapReduce module applications. The Hadoop's core components are.

1. **Hadoop Distributed File System (HDFS):** A file system that manages storage of and access the data distributed across the various nodes of a Hadoop cluster.

2. **YARN:** Hadoop cluster resource manager responsible for allocating system resources to applications and scheduling jobs.

3. **Map reduce :** A programming framework and processing engine used to run large scale batch applications in Hadoop systems.

4. **Hadoop Common :** A set of utilities and libraries that provide underlying capability required by the other pieces of Hadoop

The ecosystem that has been built up around Hadoop includes a range of other open source technologies that can complement and extend its basic capabilities. The list of related big data tools includes these examples:

- Apache Flume, a tool used to collect, aggregate and move large amounts of streaming data into HDFS;

- Apache HBase, a distributed database that's often paired with Hadoop;

- Apache Hive, a SQL-on-Hadoop tool that provides data summarization, query and analysis;

- Apache Oozie, a server-based workflow scheduling system to manage Hadoop jobs;

- Apache Phoenix, a SQL-based massively parallel processing database engine that uses HBase as its data store;

- Apache Pig, a high-level platform for creating programs that run on Hadoop clusters;

- Apache Sqoop, a tool to help transfer bulk data between Hadoop and structured data stores, such as relational databases; and

- Apache ZooKeeper, a configuration, synchronization and naming registry service for large distributed systems.

2.10.1   Hadoop Distributed File System (HDFS)

Hadoop Distributed File System (HDFS) is the primary data storage system used by Hadoop applications. It uses a name node and data node architecture to implement a distributed file system that provides high performance access to data in highly scalable Hadoop clusters. HDFS is an important part of many Hadoop ecosystem technologies because it provides a reliable means of managing large data pools and supporting related big data analytics applications. The Hadoop supports fast transfer of data between compute nodes. At its inception, it was closely integrated with MapReduce, a program framework for data processing. When HDFS takes data, it breaks the information into separate blocks and distributes it to individual nodes in the cluster, thus enabling more efficient parallel processing.

Also, Hadoop's distributed file system has been made very wrong-tolerant. The file system copies and copies each data multiple times and distributes the copy to different nodes, leaving at least one copy on the other server rack. As a result, data from crash nodes can be found elsewhere within the cluster. This ensures that processing can continue when data is retrieved. HDFS uses the master / slave architecture. The architecture is shows in the Figure 2.1. In its initial incarnation, each Hadoop cluster had a single namespace that supported file system functions and managed data storage on separate compute nodes. HDFS components support applications with large data sets.

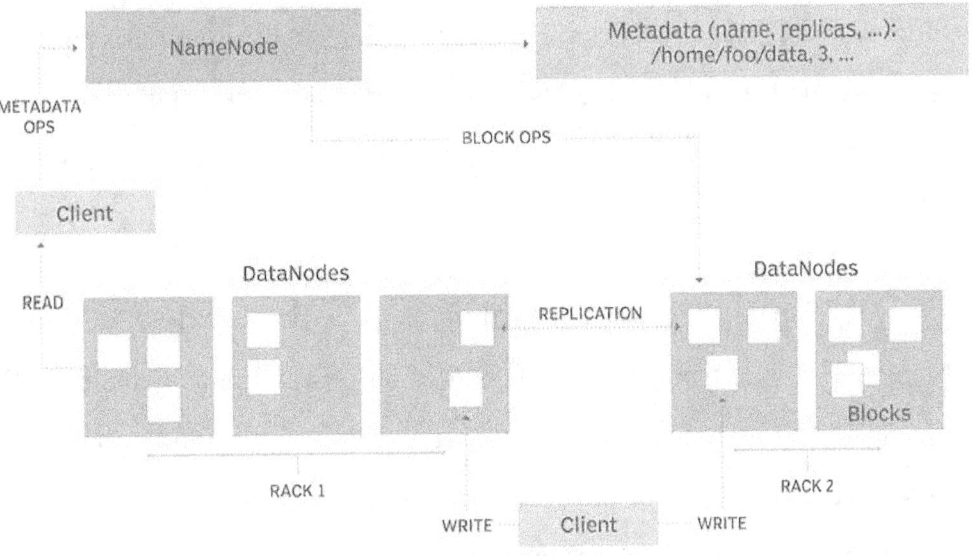

Figure 2.1 HDFS Architecture

This primary node takes the 'Data Changing' architecture because its design directs the proprietary file system outlined in Google's technical documents as well as components of IBM's General Parallel File System (GPFS) and Google File System (GFS). The system eliminates data volumes on multiple disks, by writing volumes in parallel. Although the HDFS portable operating system interface is not model-compatible, it echoes the POSIX design style in some cases. Hadoop's distributed file system originated in Yahoo as part of the company's advertising service and search engine requirements. Like other web-based companies, Yahoo has acquired a range of applications that can be accessed by a growing number of users, who are generating more and more data. Web companies that have used HDFS support big data analytics to meet these same requirements, including Facebook, eBay, LinkedIn, and Twitter. But the file system scrapped it. As part of large-scale image conversion, HDFS has created the New York Times, Media 6 Degrees for Record Processing and Machine Learning, LiveBet for Record Storage and Conflict Analysis, Jakut for Session Analysis and Fox for Record Analysis and Data Processing Used the audience network. HDFS is also at the heart of many open source data warehouse options, sometimes called data lakes.

Support for low-cost hardware is a particularly useful feature because HDFS is typically used as part of large-scale implementations. Such systems, such as running web search and related applications, for example, may have hundreds of petabytes and thousands of nodes. Server failures are common in such a way that they need to be particularly flexible. After four alpha releases and a beta, Apache Hadoop 3.0.0 was generally available in December 2017, and HDFS enhancements support additional naming, eraser coding, and greater data compression. At the same time, advances in HDFS tools, such as LinkedIn's open source Doctor Elephant and Dynamometer Performance Testing tools, have always been expanded to develop larger HDFS implementations.

2.10.2   Map Reduce

MapReduce is a programming model suitable for processing large data. Hadoop has the ability to run programs written in different languages: Java, Ruby, Python and C ++. MapReduce programs are parallel and making them very useful for analyzing large amounts of data using multiple machines in a cluster.

2.10.2.1   Phases of Map Reduce Programs

1.   Map phase

2.   Reduce phase.

Commonly an input provided to each phase is key-value pairs. Also one needs to specify two functions or programs to make it useful.

1.   map function or program

2.   reduce function Or program

2.10.2.2   Phases of execution of Map Reduce Program

The total process goes through four phases of execution. They are

1.   Splitting

The input to each map reduce process is divided into pieces called input splits with fixed size. The input split are chunk of inputs that is consumed by a single mapper.

2. Mapping

This is the basic phase in the execution process of a map reduce program. In this phase each chunk is passed to a map reduce function or program to produce the required output values. Finally it prepares a list with output values.

3. Shuffling

Here the consolidation process is taking place from the mapping phase outputs.

4. Reducing

Finally here the output values are aggregated in this final phase. This phase consolidated the values from shuffling and returns as a single output value. This phase has the responsibiity to summarize the complete data set.

2.10.2.3 MapReduce Architecture

The MapReduce Architecture consists of two trackers and two mask. One map task is created for each split which then executes map function for each record in the split. It is always beneficial to have multiple splits because the time taken to process a split is small as compared to the time taken for processing of the whole input. When the splits are smaller, the processing is better to load balanced since we are processing the splits in parallel.

However, it is also not desirable to have splits too small in size. When splits are too small, the overload of managing the splits and map task creation begins to dominate the total job execution time. For most jobs, it is better to make a split size equal to the size of a Hadoop Distributed File System (HDFS) block (which is 64 MB, by default). Execution of map tasks results into writing output to a local disk on the respective node and not to HDFS. Reason for choosing local disk over HDFS is, to avoid replication which takes place in case of HDFS store operation. The Figure 2.2 shows the architecture of Map Reducer.

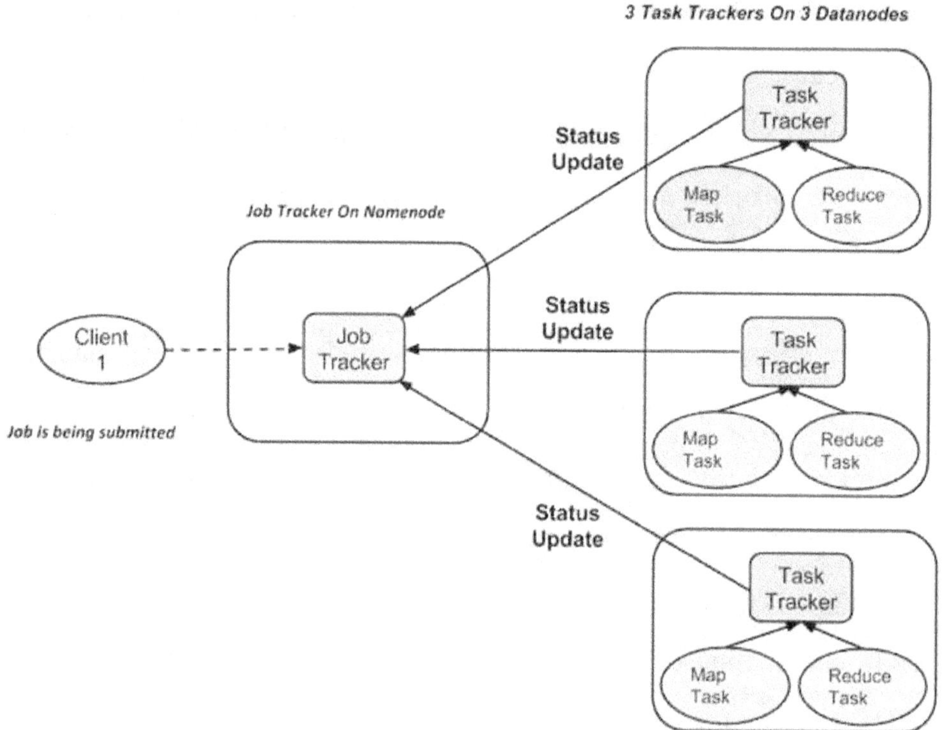

Figure 2.2 Architecture of Hadoop Map Reduce

Map output is intermediate output which is processed by reduce tasks to produce the final output. Once the job is complete, the map output can be thrown away. So, storing it in HDFS with replication becomes overkill. In the event of node failure, before the map output is consumed by the reduce task, Hadoop reruns the map task on another node and re-creates the map output. Reduce task doesn't work on the concept of data locality. An output of every map task is fed to the reduce task. Map output is transferred to the machine where reduce task is running. On this machine, the output is merged and then passed to the user-defined reduce function. Unlike the map output, reduce output is stored in HDFS (the first replica is stored on the local node and other replicas are stored on off-rack nodes). So, writing the reduce output. Hadoop divides the job into tasks. There are two types of tasks:

1. Map tasks (Splits & Mapping)

2. Reduce tasks (Shuffling, Reducing)

The complete execution process (execution of Map and Reduce tasks, both) is controlled by two types of entities called a Jobtracker: Acts like a master (responsible for complete execution of submitted job). Multiple Task Trackers: Acts like slaves, each of them performing the job. For every job submitted for execution in the system, there is one Jobtracker that resides on Namenode and there are multiple tasktrackers which reside on Datanode. A job is divided into multiple tasks which are then run onto multiple data nodes in a cluster. It is the responsibility of job tracker to coordinate the activity by scheduling tasks to run on different data nodes.

Execution of individual task is then to look after by task tracker, which resides on every data node executing part of the job. Task tracker's responsibility is to send the progress report to the job tracker. In addition, task tracker periodically sends 'heartbeat' signal to the Jobtracker so as to notify him of the current state of the system. Thus job tracker keeps track of the overall progress of each job. In the event of task failure, the job tracker can reschedule it on a different task tracker.

2.11   SUMMARY

A detailed study on the different categories of recommendation system algorithms and the methods proposed under each and every category has been done and presented here. A vast study was done to figure out how recommendation system has grown in all dimensions. Recommendation System algorithms have been evolving throughout the years. New methodologies have been proposed and experimented. The following observations were made based on the exploration of all these methodologies. 1) Recommendation System algorithms rarely identify nonexclusive data. Only few are designed to identify them. 2) Most of the location based recommendation system algorithms require the number of data to be given as input which is an important parameter that plays a crucial role in deciding the recommendation results. 3) All existing tools focus on specific Recommendation System algorithms which are very common and almost all of them perform crisp Recommendation System. 4) Existing tools lack novel algorithms. 5) Utility based Recommendation System algorithms are yet to evolve.

Analysis of these observations gave a quest for designing new techniques for location based Recommendation System data for addressing the above issues. This led to the development of a new methodology for Recommendation System. These include neural networks, Map Reduce prototypes, social innovation, user identification, and users' historical behaviours. The literature discussed here briefly describes social networking, LBSN, practices, needs, issues, location forecasting, big data, PP-KNN, and many other classification methods. Most of the current work on research work focuses on a single source of information, namely social network data or just geo-location information. Some researchers have proposed integrating information sources to improve prediction accuracy. However, they did not solve the problem of handling the data, as well as the improvement in prediction accuracy. In this sense, we propose a predictive model based on the best first gradient-based distributed tree, which handles multidimensional information and provides customized recommendations to users.

- Finding user communities requires an efficient mechanism that requires very little operational time.

- The system needs a good location ranking algorithm.

- It is known that users do not always choose their preferred locations. Therefore, the best eco-friendly method is to come up with the best places for users.

- Travel calculation requires a better algorithm. Instead of creating an itinerary in a subset of locations, the algorithm should create it in the most relevant locations where it is calculated. There is a need for a technique to improve the computed travel plans.

The recommendation system is designed to incorporate mechanisms and methods for addressing identified gaps in the domain.

CHAPTER 3

**FOURSQUARE DATASET, GRADIENT BOOSTED
DECISION TREES (GBDT) AND K-NEAREST
NEIGHBOUR (KNN) CLASSIFIERS**

The existence of plenty of methods for recommendation system for location based data can be inferred from the literature review presented in the previous chapter. This chapter dwells on a few well known, notable recommendation system algorithms that have been repeatedly used in the literature and/or recently proposed. This chapter outlines the interesting concepts, design techniques and drawbacks of some of the existing methodologies. Some concepts of these algorithms have been adopted in the proposed framework.

3.1 INTRODUCTION

Most of recommendation system algorithms categorized as content based, collaborative, utility based and hybrid recommendation system algorithms perform crisp recommendation system on the datasets. Crisp recommendation system is based on mathematical crisp sets and this type of recommendation system places an object or a location in exactly one cluster. K-means, K-medoids are best examples of crisp recommendation system. This type of crisp recommendation system does not suit for location based data because location data have tendency to participate in multiple location based process and such algorithms do not have the ability to adapt to different user requirements on cluster granularity for different subsets of the data.

Moreover noisy data in the for location based matrix will have impact on the clusters during crisp recommendation system.

On the other hand, Fuzzy recommendation system, a soft computing methodology uses fuzzy techniques to cluster data with an aim to exploit the tolerance for imprecision, uncertainty, approximate reasoning and partial truth. This technique considers an object to be grouped in more than one cluster. This type of algorithms leads to recommendation system schemes that can handle the uncertainty of real data. The most important fuzzy recommendation system algorithm is Fuzzy C-Means Bezdeck *et al.* (1984). In the case of fuzzy membership, each location data belongs to a cluster with a membership weight between 0, (definitely excluded), and 1, (definitely included). Though there are plenty of techniques available for performing crisp or fuzzy recommendation system we would like to dwell on a few notable and/or recently proposed algorithms for recommendation system for location based data.

3.2 EXISTING METHODOLOGIES AND THEIR DRAWBACKS- AN OVERVIEW

The most common and widely known method for recommendation system is the K-means algorithm. K-means is a partition based method which groups objects into clusters depending on the distance or similarity between the objects and cluster centroid. The number of clusters, say n, expected as output needs to be specified in advance. Initially the centroid values for all n clusters are assigned randomly. For each object present in the dataset, the distance/similarity between the object and the centroid of a cluster is found. The distance is measured using Euclidean distance and there are also other similarity measures available. The Euclidean distance between objects (gi,gj) can be given as in Equation (3.1).

$$d(gi, gj) = \sqrt{\Sigma_k (x_{ik} - x_{jk})^2} \tag{3.1}$$

Input: No of clusters and the Location data expression dataset

1. Initialize k cluster centers randomly
2. Calculate the distance between the objects and the center using the similarity metric
3. Assign objects to the nearest cluster
4. Find new cluster centers
5. Iterate until no change in cluster centers

Figure 3.1 Design steps in K-means algorithm

The object is assigned to the cluster whose centroid is nearest to the object. After all assignments are made, the new cluster centroids are calculated which is usually the mean of all objects in the cluster. This process iterates until there is no change in the cluster centroids. As we see in the process, the k-means procedure has four important steps: Initialization, Assignment, Formation of clusters, Iteration. The Pseudo code of K-means algorithm is shown in Figure 3.1.

The Rough K-means algorithm proposed by Lingras & West (2004) provides a rough set theoretic flavour to the conventional K-means algorithm to deal with uncertainty involved in cluster analysis. The rough K-means algorithm works similar to K-means but represents a cluster with lower and upper approximations. For this the distance between an object and all cluster centroids is calculated. The object is assigned to the cluster based on the ratio between the minimum distance and the other distance. (ie) For each object v, let $d(v,x_i)$ be the distance between itself and the centroid of cluster x_i. The difference between $d(v,x_i) - d(v,x_j)$. $1 \leq i,\ j \leq k$ is used to determine the membership of object v as follows:

- If $d(v,x_i) - d(v,x_j) \leq$ threshold, then $v \in U(x_i)$ &$v \in U(x_j)$. ie.,(Upper bound of x_i and x_j). Furthermore, v will not be a part of any lower bound.

- Otherwise, $v \in L(x_i)$, such that $d(v,x_i)$ is the minimum for $1 \leq i \leq k$. In addition, $v \in U(x_i)$.

Input: Number of clusters and the Location data expression dataset

1. Select an initial cluster of n objects into k clusters.
2. Calculate the distance between the objects and the center.
3. Assign each object to the Lower bound ($L(x)$) or upper bound ($U(x)$) of clusters respectively
4. Find new cluster center based on the weighted combination of the data points in its lower_bound and upper_bound.
5. Iterate until no change in cluster centers

Figure 3.2 Design steps of Rough K-means algorithm

One main drawback of k-means and Rough k-means when applied on for location based data is that it requires the number of clusters to be specified prior to recommendation system. This exact number is very difficult to decide upon. The smaller the number, a very few large clusters would result. The larger the number, the algorithm will end producing large number of small clusters. The exact number of clusters actually depends on the given dataset. Moreover, both algorithms use Euclidean distance as similarity metric which makes them less efficient in capturing co-regulated location data with similar expression patterns. K-means perform crisp recommendation system.

3.3 EXISTING METHODOLOGIES

Some of the recommendation system's algorithms described above or discussed in chapter 2 are published with available implementations, in the form of methodology. Several recommendation system algorithms have been compiled and implemented for comparison with other methods or to make

Recommendation system a more available methodology for others in the field. In this section, a brief description of some of the most interesting methodology is presented.

3.4 NEED FOR THE STUDY

As an outcome of the exhaustive analysis done on the existing algorithms and tools, the following observations were made.

1) Most of the recommendation system algorithms perform crisp recommendation system. The main problem with For location based data analysis is uncertainty and crisp recommendation system algorithm can hardly capture the uncertainties associated with the data.

2) Most of the cluster algorithms require the number of clusters to be specified for recommendation system to be done on the dataset. It is very difficult for the user to know the number of clusters existing in the dataset and the parameter 'number of clusters' plays a vital role in deciding the cluster results.

3) Many recommendation system algorithms do not identify nonexclusive clusters. Location data usually participate in multiple locations and recommendation system algorithms that produce exclusive (non-overlapping) clusters/ bi-clusters cannot identify location data that participate in multiple processes. Recommendation system algorithms that produce nonexclusive (overlapping) clusters and bi-clusters would be more suitable for recommendation system for location based data.

4) All the existing methodologies offer only crisp recommendation system algorithms researchers to use. Rough and fuzzy based recommendation system methodologies are not readily available for use in existing tools.

The above mentioned setbacks in the existing methodologies gave a quest to design a suite of algorithms for recommendation system for location based data. As Rough sets provide a mathematical framework for capturing uncertainty associated with for location based data, a suite of algorithms based on Rough sets for recommendation system for location based data was developed. The Proposed system addresses all the issues mentioned above.

3.5 THE PROPOSED NOVEL SUITE

The main focus of the research work is to develop rough sets based recommendation system algorithms that can efficiently handle the uncertainties associated with for location based data. This led to the development of KNN based classifier which is actually a suite of four novel recommendation system based on rough set theory for recommendation system for location based data to rectify the setbacks.

The structure of the proposed KNN Based optimal travel recommendation system is given in Figure 3.3. It has three different categories: Social Innovation, Location Recommendation and Travel Recommendation. Each component serves a well-defined purpose towards efficient location and travel recommendations. Social innovation is first performed and the elements are continuously distorted with location suggestion, travel calculation and finally, travel recommendation. An overview of the three sections of each is given in the subsequent sections.

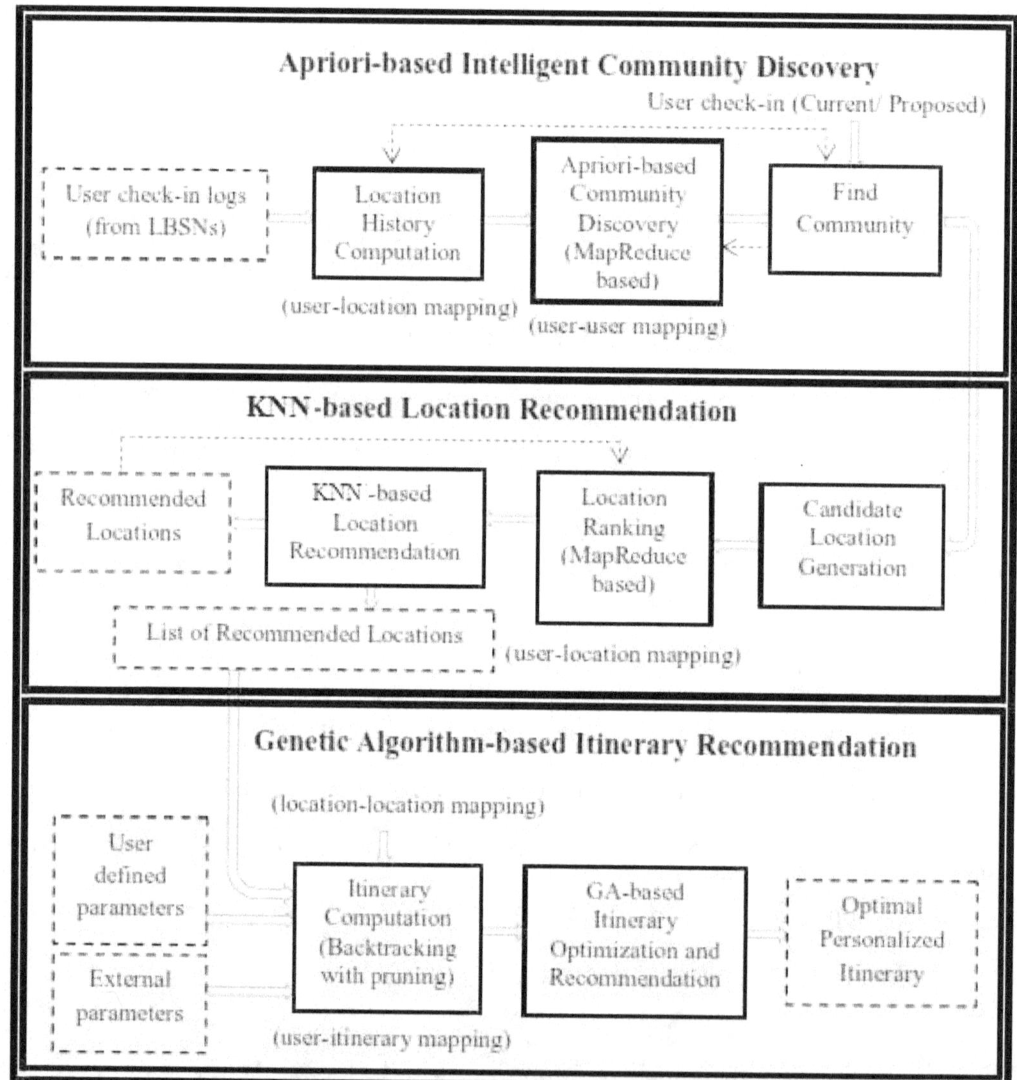

Figure 3.3   Architecture of the KNN Based optimized itinerary recommendation system

The input to the system for generating the user's location history is provided to the Social Innovation module. This input is collected from the location-based social network Foursquare. Foursquare data is collected from Twitter messages using TwitterAPI. When a new user checks in a location or proposes to move, the system calculates the communities the user falls into when requesting a location or travel suggestion.

User's friends are identified from the communities involved. Candidate seats for the nomination are determined and weights assigned to them. Tips or suggestions provided by users at the candidate locations are collected and these places are ranked, followed by the input of a KNN based classifier to determine the appropriate locations to suggest to the user. These destinations are then sent to the travel accounting algorithm, which calculates potential trips from these destinations. Calculated travel plans are enhanced by a GA-based approach to efficient recommendation.

The framework is designed to provide a GUI interface through which the users will be able to provide the input parameters and other specifications. There is a provision to choose one of the algorithms and to display the recommendation system output. The suite provides an interactive interface for clearly displaying bi-clusters along with the location data and conditions that fall in each bi-cluster. The effective functioning mechanism of all the algorithms is explained clearly in the following chapters.

3.6   DATASET

Foursquare is the most popular LBSN dataset (Narayanan & Serikuri 2016; Floyer 2013) which examines the user's check-in behavior and social history relationships among LBSNs. The user's check-in history is treated with timestamps in the Foursquare Database with his / her friendly information. For collecting user check-ins, Foursquare does not have a public utility program interface (API) where the history of the check-in is not directly obtained. But the user's check-in messages are posted on Twitter as tweets, and are accessed through Twitter's public API. It has a unique URL that points to the Foursquare webpage that contains the geographic information of the user's check-in location. From August 2010 to November 2011, checks with timestamps were considered. To maintain friendship with Foursquare data, the Foursquare user's social circle was used directly from Foursquare. In our study, users with at least ten check-ins were considered (Liu *et al.* ., 2017). A total of 43,108 geographical locations were obtained as location vocabulary. In this dataset, the user's location is stored with the latitude reference. The data from the dataset are as follows: 18,107; No. Checks: 2,073,740 and no. Links: 115,574. This dataset contains information about: Foursquare users' check-in information; Foursquare's user-friendly network; And Foursquare users' home location.

3.7   GRADIENT BOOSTED DECISION TREES

A tree as a data structure has many analogies in real life. It is used in many areas because it is a good representation of a decision-making process. The tree contains the root node, the end node, and the node node (nodes, which are not further separated). Trees are usually drawn upside down, which means the leaves are at the base of the tree. Result trees can be used for both regression and classification problems. The decision trees show good results in non-linear functions. In the example above, it can be seen that the dividing surface of each class is constant and that each side of the surface is parallel to the coordinate axis. Slope ascent is known as one of the leading ensemble mechanisms. Increasing the slope The slope descent is used to improve the loss function. There are several gradient boosting libraries:

XGiBoost, H20, LightGPM. The main difference between them only in tree structure, feature engineering and working with sparse data.

GBDT is an additive regression model consisting of numerous weak decision tree learners $h_i(x)$ as in Equation (3.10):

$$H_k(x) = \sum_{i=1}^{k} \gamma_i h_i(x) \qquad (3.10)$$

where γ_i denotes the learning rate.

During the progression of gradient boosting, weighted resampling is accepted to place weight on observations which are harder to calculate exactly. If a new regression tree is included, then the value of each opinion is re-calculated. The result can be allotted such that low estimated accuracy is allocated to a higher weight. After completion of an iteration, the sampling weight is reorganised. The remarks with lower accuracy can be experimented with higher probability at the next iteration. The input variables are seldom of equal relevance for the prediction performance, and usually only some of them have substantial influence on the model output (Yang *et al.* ., 2017).

3.8 SUMMARY

A few notable, recent methodologies used for recommendation system for location based data were presented in this chapter. The following observations were made based on the exploration of all these methodologies. 1) Recommendation system algorithms rarely identify nonexclusive clusters. Only few are designed to identify them. 2) Most of the cluster algorithms require the number of clusters to be given as input which is an important parameter that plays a crucial role in deciding the cluster results. 3) All existing methodologies focus on specific recommendation system algorithms which are very common and almost all of them perform crisp recommendation system. 4) Existing methodologies lack novel algorithms based on fuzzy or rough sets.5) Rough set based recommendation system algorithms are yet to evolve.

Analysis of these observations gave a quest for designing new techniques for recommendation system for location based data for addressing the above issues. This led to the development of a new framework with all new algorithms for recommendation system. The overall system for travel and location recommendation may meet the thrown requirements and handle features that are not present in the current referral system.

CHAPTER 4

BEST FIRST GRADIENT BOOSTED DISTRIBUTED DECISION TREE BASED ONLINE LOCATION BASED SERVICES FROM USER ACTIVITY

4.1   INTRODUCTION

Raising the slope tree creates an additive regression model, using decision trees as a weak learner. While this is certainly the case for GBDT, decision trees in general have an advantage in other learners making a lot of sense. GBDT is highly adaptable and can be used for a variety of damage operations. More recently, gamete optimization of GBDT using rank-specific loss functions has been effective in improving search matching. In addition to its advantages in interpreting, it is possible to perform feature selection naturally by modeling GBDT feature interactions. In addition to the use of surface decision trees, trees in random GBDT are trained in a subset of randomly chosen training data and are less likely to be more fitting. However, as we try to include a large number of features and events in the training data, we focus our attention on the distribution of the GBDT algorithm, as all existing training data must be in physical memory.

In this work, we present a non-distributed distributed random GBDT algorithm that produces trees similar to those trained by the non-distributed method. Our distributed approach is also common for GBDT derivatives. We focus on modifying the structure of incentives with extensive decision tree learning. In our work, we explore two different techniques for parallelizing random GBDTs in Hadoop 1. Both methods depend on improving the training time of individual trees, but not on changing the actual excitation phase. Our initial effort focuses on the implementation of reducing the original map and our second approach uses a new way to begin work on Hadoop.

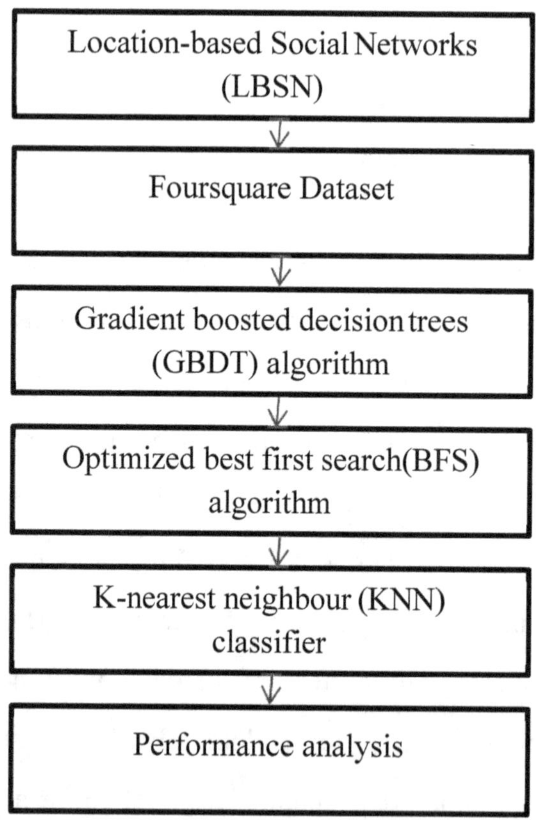

Figure 4.1   Flow diagram of proposed work

The system is intended to provide users with the optimal travel itinerary, which is timely recommended. The surveyed literature has revealed that current systems do not have the best methods of social innovation, such as location ranking, location recommendation, travel calculation, and methods for improving travel plans. In addition to responding to requests for referrals in a very short time, the system can also integrate cold startup issues and methods for dealing with data gaps.

The recommendation system is tailored to the methods of overcoming these problems. Key algorithms are implemented using the Hadoop and Map Reduce programming example for faster responses. The system is proposed as a hybrid referral system, combining the essence of joint filtering and content based systems. It considers the implicit ratings of customers and their friends as the primary standard of referrals, thus creating a common filter component of the referral system. Tips or hints will be considered on potential locations offered by other users to improve suggestions. Profile matching is done to solve the cold start problem and these make up the content-oriented part of the referral system.

Therefore, user location history, tips left by users at these locations, and key inputs of the user environment system, is a complete travel recommendation system. It provides suggestions on the context and past behavior of individuals calculated from location history. Furthermore, it contributes to customized or customized aggregations, which increase diversity referrals in sources or input interests.

The structure of the proposed flow diagram is given in Figure 4.1. It has six different categories. Each component provides a well-defined advantage over the effective location and travel recommendations. Social innovation needs to be done first, followed by constantly distorted factors such as location recommendation, travel computation and finally travel recommendation. An overview of each of the three sections is given in the next sections.

The input to the system is provided to the Social Innovation Module to create a user location history. This input is collected from a location-based social network Foursquare. Foursquare data is extracted from Twitter messages using TwitterAPI. When a new user checks in or proposes to move, the system calculates the number of communities the user will fall into when requesting a location or travel recommendation.

Identify user friends from participating communities. Candidate seats for the nomination will be decided and the weights assigned to them. Tips or suggestions provided by users in the candidate positions are collected and these places are ranked, followed by the input of the KNN based classification to determine the appropriate locations to point to the user. These destinations are then sent to the travel accounting algorithm, which calculates the potential journeys from these destinations. Travel plans calculated through a GA-based approach to effective referral can be enhanced.

4.2 PHASES IN THE PROPOSED SYSTEM

4.2.1 Location Based Social Networks (LBSN)

There may be common interests and behaviors. Similarity between users inferred from location histories can enable friend suggestions, which also connect users with similar interests. Social innovation is a group of people who share common interests while they may not have known each other before.

1. Finding Local Experts in a Region: With the locations of users, we are able to identify local professionals who have a richer knowledge about one region than others. Their travel experiences, e.g., The places they were in were very

responsible and valuable for travel. For example, local experts know more about high quality restaurants than some tourists.

2. Social Innovation: Using these assumptions from users 'locations, these users are grouped together and share common interests such as users visiting museums. As a result, a person can easily initiate a group activity such as raising or buying tickets at a group price by sending invitations to appropriate users on a social site.

4.2.1.1 Understanding Locations

Here, we focus on understanding locations based on user information.

1. General Travel Recommendations

- Mining the most interesting places: Finding the most interesting places in a city and the travel scenes in between is a common task a tourist wants to accomplish when travel to an unfamiliar city. Location-based social networks allow us to identify such information by mining the location histories of a large number of users.

- Travel Planning: Sometimes a sophisticated journey is required by the user's travel time and departure location. The itinerary includes not only individual destinations, but also detailed routes and proper schedules for connecting these destinations, e.g., the usual time of day for most people to arrive and the appropriate length of time a tourist should stay.

- Location-Functional Referrer: This recommendation provides two types of recommendations to a user: 1) the most popular activities that can be done in a given location and 2) the most popular places to run a given activity, such as shopping. These two types of suggestions can be cut from numerous user trends and location-coded comments.

2.	**Personalized Travel Suggestions**

- User-Based Joint Filtering: In this scenario, the similarity between each pair of users (introduced above) is incorporated into a joint filtering model to run a customized location recommendation system, which provides locations that match a person's preferences. The general idea behind collective filtering [23, 30] is that similar users vote similarly on similar products. Therefore, if similarity is determined between users and items, predictions can be made about the user's potential ratings of those items. For example, if we know that user A and B are Very similar (based on their location histories), we can suggest locations where user A already has user B.

- Location-Based Joint Filtering: User-based Joint Filtering can accurately shape a person's behavior. However, because the model has to calculate the similarity between each pair of users, it suffers from an increasing number of users (in a real system). To solve this problem, location-based joint filtration is proposed. This model treats a location as an object and calculates the relationship between locations based on the location histories of the users visiting these locations. As for the limited geographical location (i.e., the number of locations is limited), this location-based model is more practical for a real system. The main challenge of a location-based model is how to create a behavior that is beneficial to a user-based model.

- Events innovation from social media A few projects aim to detect conflicting events, such as concerts, traffic accidents, sales promotions and festivals, using media (such as geo-encoded photos and tweets) posted by a large number of users on a location-based social network. Intuitively, people who see such an event post a significant amount of media (eg, tweets) at the event Occurs. By compiling and mining media in conjunction with specific locations, we can automatically get a feel for geo-social events.

4.2.1.2   Input Data Generation

Important input data for prior knowledge on what proposals the popular and widely accepted LBSN, user check-in registration extracted from Foursquare. Foursquare users can check-in at various places and share their check-ins on Twitter or Facebook. Although Foursquare provides an API for data extraction, users must meet certain authentication criteria. Most current systems that use Four square user data extract Twitter messages using TwitterApp. This method follows the same procedure. For the purpose of analysis, the system also used user data from Covalla and BrideKit, which can be downloaded free of charge from the Stanford University website, from which the location history of each user is calculated.

4.2.2   Best First Search(BFS)

The best first search algorithm works based on the framework of Rough sets. In the context of clustering, location based matrix is considered as a large matrix of continuous expression values of location data under different experimental conditions. The status of the cellular process and the similarity of the location based data can be found by identifying the patterns hidden in the expression profile. Correlation coefficient as a similarity metric for clustering gives better outcome on continuous data like location data (Cluster Analysis). Moreover Pearson's correlation coefficient is widely used and has been proved efficient as a similarity measure for location based data (Jiang *et al.* 2004, Anindya *et al.* 2009). So the algorithm best first search was designed to use Pearson's correlation coefficient as the metric for finding the similarity matrix. With the help of the similarity matrix the initial assignments to clusters are done. Each object v is either assigned to the upper or the lower approximation of a cluster. The mean of each cluster (lower and upper) is then taken as the centre of that cluster.

The step 1 of the algorithm finds out the possible number of clusters and the similarity matrix. For each activity g_i, it finds the similarity between all other activites g_j and g_i. Correlation coefficient is used as the metric to construct the similarity matrix. Equation (4.1) gives the Pearson's correlation coefficient for measuring the similarity between two activities (x_i, x_j).

$$f_{sim}(x_i, x_j) = \sum_{l=1}^{m}(x_{il} - \bar{x}_i)(x_{jl} - \bar{x}_j)/\sqrt{\sum_{l=1}^{m}(x_{il} - \bar{x}_i)^2 \sum_{l=1}^{m}(x_{jl} - \bar{x}_j)^2}$$

$$(4.1)$$

If the similarity value is greater than the correlation threshold α, then both the activities are considered to be similar and are placed in the same cluster. If they are not similar, place them in different clusters and increment the number of clusters by 1. By the end of step 1, we will have the possible number of clusters k and the similarity matrix. The initial assignments of objects to the clusters are done using the similarity matrix. This initial assignment based on the correlation between the data helps us to generate more meaningful clusters. The location data like information about a town or city that are more similar are put in the same cluster. The cluster centroid for each cluster is considered to be the mean of that cluster objects.

Now, for each object P in the given dataset, the similarity or distance between the object P and all the k cluster centroids is calculated. Out of the k similarity, let the similarity between P and the jth cluster be the maximum. For each cluster i, the ratio between the maximum similarity (similarity with the jth cluster) and similarity of the ith cluster is generated. This ratio R, the ratio between the maximum similarity (similarity with the jth cluster) and similarity of the ith cluster is found using Equation (4.2).

$$R = \frac{d(P,m_j)}{d(P,m_i)} \qquad (4.2)$$

If this ratio R is less than a specified membership threshold β, then the cluster i is added to the set A. This step is repeated for all clusters. Finally the set A is analysed. If $A = \emptyset$ then the object P is assigned to the lower approximation of cluster i (the one with the maximum similarity). If A is not empty, then the object P is assigned to the boundary region of all the clusters that are elements of set A. The elements in the lower and boundary region together form the upper approximation of the clusters.

The new mean of each cluster (lower and upper) is then taken as the centroid of that cluster and is computed as given in Equation (4.3).

$$C_i = w_l \frac{\sum_{v \in \underline{C_i}} v}{|\underline{C_i}|} + w_u \frac{\sum_{v \in \overline{C_j}} v}{|\overline{C_j}|} \tag{4.3}$$

The parameters w_l and w_u determine the importance of lower and upper approximation and $w_l + w_b = 1$. The process iterates and dynamically updates the similarity matrix until there is no more change in the cluster centroid. The final results will include the number of clusters existing in the dataset and the group of activities in the upper and lower approximation of each and every cluster.

4.2.2.1 Best-First Search Algorithm using OPEN/CLOSED List

The optimized BFS algorithm is used to optimize the number of iterations and Shrinkage using best first algorithm. Best-first search is a search algorithm which explores a graph by expanding the most promising node chosen according to a specified rule. BFS is a traversing algorithm where you should start traversing from a selected node (source or starting node) and traverse the graph layer wise thus exploring the neighbour nodes (nodes which are directly connected to source node). You must then move towards the next-level neighbour nodes. As the name BFS suggests, you are required to traverse the graph breadthwise as follows: First move horizontally and visit all the nodes of the current layer Move to the next layer.

A general BFS algorithm is presented here. Two sets are used, OPEN and CLOSED, where in OPEN unexpanded nodes are stored and in CLOSED expanded nodes. Three operations, pop(S), push(n, S) and remove(n, S), are assumed for a node n and a set S. pop(S) operation tries to select a single node from S, push(n, S) stores the node n into S and remove(n, S) removes n from S if n is already stored. According to sorting strategy OPEN is sorted and the best node is returned according to the strategy by the selected pop(S).

Every sorting strategy is denoted as a vecotro of a number of sorting criteria such as [criterion1, criterion2, . . ., criterionk], which defines a lexicographic ordering, i.e., from the OPEN list, first, select a set of nodes using criterion1, and if there are still multiple nodes remaining in the set, then break ties using criterion2 and so on, until a single node is selected.

The first-level sorting criterion of a strategy is criterion1, the second-level sorting criterion is criterion2, and so on. Using this notation, A * without any tie-breaking strategy can be denoted as a BFS with [f] and A * which breaks ties according to h value is denoted as [f, h]. Unless stated otherwise, it is assumed that the nodes are sorted in the increasing order of the key value and the smallest key value is selected by BFS.

Best-First Search Algorithm

Input : , *is _ goal*$(.)$ *successors* .$(\ )$

Initialize OPEN $= \varnothing, CLOSED = \varnothing, g(n_0) = 0,\ (\forall_n \neq n_0 ; g(n) = \infty)$

push$(n_0,\ OPEN\ )$

while OPEN $\neq \varnothing$ do

n=pop(OPEN);push(n,CLOSED)

return n if is_goal(n)=true

for each m $\in$ successors(n) do

  $g_{new} = g(n) + \cos t(n, m)$

 if $g_{new} < g(m)$*then*

   g(m) $\leftarrow$ g_{new} ; *parent*(m) $\leftarrow$ *n; push(m,OPEN); remove(m, CLOSED)*

Figure 4.2   Best-First Search Algorithm using OPEN/CLOSED List

However, only a partial ordering is provided a sorting strategy, i.e., the sorting strategy may fail to select a single node because some nodes may share the same sorting keys. For such cases, a BFS algorithm must decide which node to expand by applying some default tie-breaking criterion criterion k which is guaranteed to return a single node, such as FIFO (oldest node first: first-in-first out), LIFO (most recently inserted first: last-in-first-out) ro (random ordering). The worst case time complexity of best first search is $O(b^m)$. Where, m is the Maximum depth of the search space and b is the branch factor.

4.2.3   k-nearest Neighbor (k-NN)

The k-nearest neighbor (k-NN) query is one of the most important query types for location based services (LBS). Various methods have been proposed to efficiently process the k-NN query. However, most of the existing methods suffer from high computation time and larger memory requirement because they unnecessarily access cells to find the nearest cells on a index.

A k-NN query can be applied to many LBS applications. To get the result of a k-NN query, it searches cells overlapped with a certain rectangle while extending the size of its all sides such as top, down, right, and left until the initial k-NN is found. The time complexity of kNN algorithm for the brute-force neighbour search is O(nXm) where n is the number of training examples and m is the number of dimensions in the training set.

4.3   SUMMARY

The overall system for travel and location recommendation may meet the thrown requirements and handle features that are not present in the current recommendation system. The overall system performance for travel and location recommendation has been found to be very satisfactory, overcoming almost all the shortcomings associated with current systems for the same application.

CHAPTER 5

PERFORMANCE EVALUATION OF BEST FIRST GRADIENT BOOSTED DISTRIBUTED DECISION TREE MODEL

The proposed new model, Best First Gradient Boosted Distributed Decision Tree, groups location data into bi-clusters based on rough set theory. This chapter discusses in detail the framework of the bi-clustering model designed as part of the suite. The architecture, design, description and the results of the proposed model are presented here. The proposed model is applied on different datasets and the results are evaluated, analyzed and compared.

5.1 INTRODUCTION

Travel recommendation system is one that recommends a user to a destination built from a place, in most cases, a town. Interested users can use the system for travel and find suitable location suggestions for their needs. If a user is new to a place, our proposed system may help him or her to recommend suitable places or help him or her to find a suitable place to cross town locations if they want to cross town locations.

This type of referral system considers the user's travel history and the history of his friends to determine locations or particular point of interest. Travel history is nothing but the order of places visited by the user, with details such as arrival time, they can be limited to the same town or different places. It is known that people's behavior in the past and present affects their acceptance of their places in the future. This historical behavior, when gathered from social networks, contributes to more accurate and possibility of getting accurate results. The user environment is concerned with the suggestion that he or she changes with the environment when a travel plan is created for him or her.

It aims to provide optimal travel for computer users, which is recommended from time to time. The surveyed literature shows that current systems do not have the best methods of social innovation like page ranking, such as location ranking, location recommendations, travel calculations and ways to improve travel plans. In addition to responding to requests for recommendations in a very short time, the system can integrate cold start issues and methods for dealing with data gaps.

5.2 DESIGN MODEL OF PROPOSED METHODOLOGY

The recommendation method is designed to fit with the methods of overcoming these problems. The dominant algorithm is implemented using the Hadoop graph mapping programming paradigm for faster responses. The aim of the proposed user recommendation system is to improve the accuracy and provide greater satisfaction to the user while they access the social network. The survey expose that most of the related systems did not give focus on implementing the more accurate classifier and choosing the relevant social network from predicted tags by capturing the users current interest. In the proposed system, KNN algorithm is adapted into the classifier which classifies the current user navigation to the best profitable navigation profile. Sometimes, the closeness between the classified navigation profiles creates the uncertainty situation in the prediction. This uncertainty situation is better handled in the recommendation engine by capturing the current interest of social network user and filter out the predicted navigation that are irrelevant to the current interest of user. The system is proposed as a hybrid referral system, which combines the essence of integrated filtering-based and content-based systems. It considers the implicit ratings of users and their friends as the primary criteria for referrals, thus forming an integrated filtering area of the referral system. Suggestions or suggestions of potential locations offered by other users are considered to improve the recommendations. Profiles fit to deal with the cold start problem, and are a content-based part of the referral system.

Increasing the slope tree produces additive regression models, using decision trees as weak learners. Although this is the best first GBDT, it is usually meaningful because decision trees have an advantage over other learners. Improved First GBDT is very usable and can be used for a variety of damage activities. Recently, improved first-order GBDT optimization using pairwise and improved specific loss functions has been shown to improve search matching. In addition to its advantages in explaining, one can naturally select a feature by first modeling the GBDT feature interactions. In addition to the use of surface decision trees, trees in GBDT are first trained in a subset of randomly selected training data and are not affected by large numbers. However, as we attempt to include incremental features and events in the training data, we first focus our attention on the distribution of the GBDT algorithm, as all existing training data must be in physical memory.

Here, we present a distributed best-in-class GBDT algorithm as a criterion for producing trees similar to those trained by the non-distributed method. In our distribution, the approach is also common to GBDT derivatives. We focus on changing the structure of offers with comprehensive decision tree learning. In our work, we first explore two different techniques for parallelizing GBDT in Hadoop. Both methods rely on improving the training time of individual trees, but not on changing the actual excitation phase. Our initial effort focused on the original. Map Reduction Implementation and our second approach use a new way to start MPI jobs in Hadoop. The main role of the log system is to prepare the usage data of social network which is available in the form log file for the web usage mining. When the recommendation engine receives the competing future navigation pattern from the classifier as input, it employs the location based Updation and rank scoring algorithm to resolve the competition and recommends the relevant locations as future navigation to the user in the descending order of rank score. Here, the need for implementing the concept score update propagation algorithm is to capture the current user interest in the social network. The inputs for algorithm are LSW and social network profile.

The social network profile is built where the entire knowledge of the social network is represented in the hierarchical form of location concepts and sub location concepts using the 'is a' and 'part of 'relations. When the user interacts with the social network by accessing a location, user gets the instance of social network profile. Each concept is commented with score of one. Then, update propagation algorithm is used to update the score of concept commented with each concept of social network profile instance based on the current navigation of social network user. With the help of the social network profile instance, user current interest is always tracked and used to make the prediction of locations relevant to the current user interest. location concept score based similarity comparison algorithm in recommendation engine receives updated social network profile which is the output of the concept update propagation algorithm and all the predicted locations from classification module. This algorithm is used to filter out the predicted locations which are irrelevant to the current user interest and rank the predicted locations relevant to user based on the rank score. Finally, predicted locations are recommended to the social network user in the descending order of rank score.

In parallel to our decision tree training process, training data should be distributed between machines. Instead of copying to reduce memory usage, we are only interested in ways to share data on different systems. There are already several approaches to distributed tree building that aim to improve scaling and training performance in terms of memory usage. Gorgia and. Al. Distributed tree training methods and different methods of sharing training data horizontally or vertically. In our work, we distributed our data using vertically and horizontally distributed systems.

The efficiency of a clustering or bi-clustering algorithm not only depends on the ability to find actual structure existing in the given data but also lies in the quality of the clusters or bi-cluster (i.e) how close objects are within the same partition and how far from the rest. Cluster validation is the process of assessing the quality and reliability of the cluster sets derived from various clustering techniques. The quality of a cluster is mainly decided based on the similarity of the objects within a cluster (homogeneity) and the dissimilarity between two different clusters (separation).

The best first gradient boosted distributed decision tree based model which consists of few algorithms based on rough sets was experimented with different location based datasets and the results were analyzed. The performance of the proposed algorithms when experimented with different bench marked datasets was found to be very promising. The resulting clusters and bi-clusters were validated. The results of the validation and the implementation of the model is presented in detail.

In reality, location data tend to be co-regulated and co-expressed under only a few experimental conditions. They may start behaving differently under different conditions. If a given dataset has many experimental conditions and if an algorithm tries to find out group of location data expressed similarly under all experimental conditions, and then the algorithm will be rarely successful in finding such a group. This is because clustering algorithms group location data on a single dimension, either row or column. When clustering algorithms are used, each location data in a given location d ata cluster is defined using all the conditions. Similarly, each condition in a condition cluster is characterized by the activity of all the location data. But in bi-clustering, each location data is selected using only a subset of the conditions and each condition is selected using only a subset of the location data. Bi-clustering performs clustering in both the dimensions simultaneously. This gave the quest to develop a new rough set based bi-clustering algorithm which will perform clustering on both dimensions (row and column) simultaneously and produce clusters with upper and lower approximation that helps in better interpretation of results. The goal of this bi-clustering algorithm is to identify subgroups of location data and subgroups of conditions, by performing simultaneous clustering of both rows and columns of the location data matrix, instead of clustering these two dimensions separately as done in GBDT. Increasing the gradient tree creates an additive regression model, using decision trees as a weak learner. While this is arguably the best first GBDT, it is generally understandable because decision-making trees have an advantage over other learners. Better first GBDT is more usable and can be used for a variety of loss functions. More recently, better first-order GBDT adaptations using pairwise and ranking specific loss functions have been shown to improve search fit. The main advantage of GBDT method over the previous method is that GBDT location data rates only clusters whereas GBDT location data rates bi-clusters. The design architecture of GBDT algorithm is given in Figure 5.1

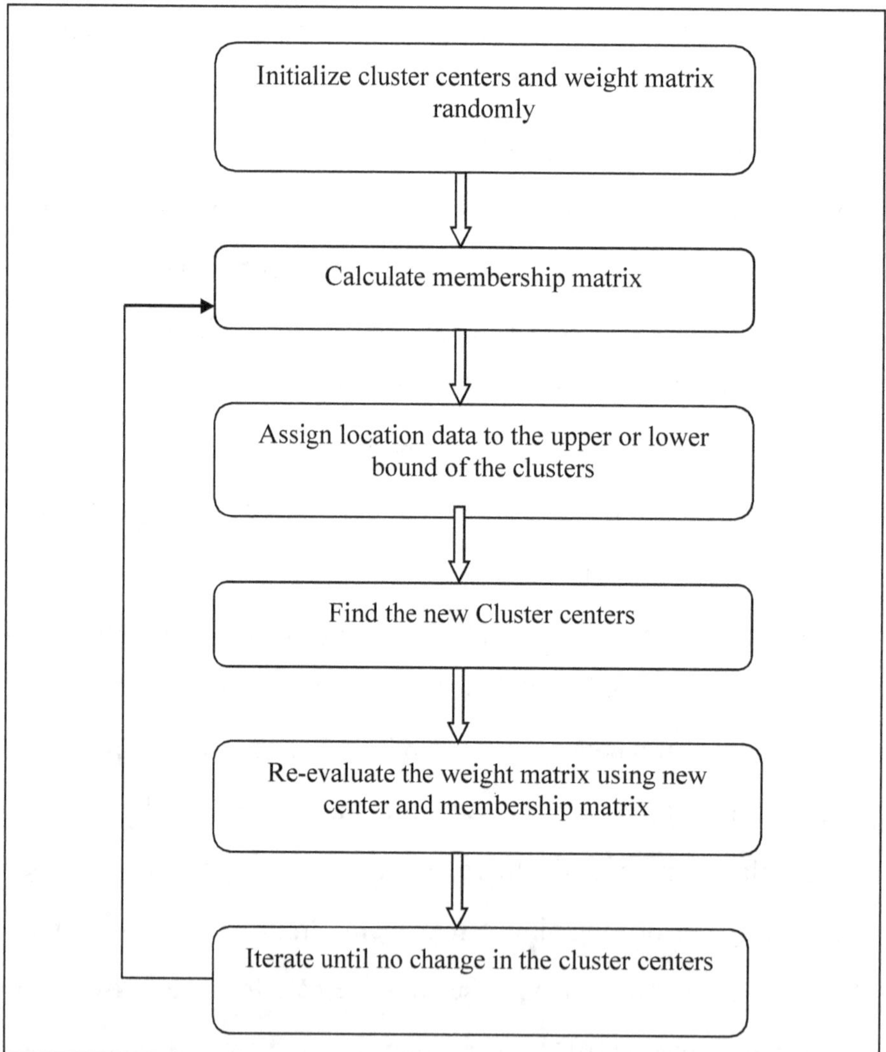

Figure 5.1　**The Design Model of best first gradient boosted distributed decision tree**

Our initial implementation of distributed decision trees attempted to create a problem with the Map Reduce paradigm and used a horizontal sharing approach. We proposed the concept of combining attribute, value, and class label pairs, which we used in our Map Reduce implementation. For tree construction, mappers will collect sufficient statistics, where each computes candidate cut-offs by assembling unique attribute-value pairs. Most of the existing traditional algorithms like k-means, hierarchical, clique and many others presented in the previous chapter require the user to specify the number of location data or group.

This is very difficult because the user will not be aware of the number of groups in the given dataset. As the number of groups plays a crucial role in deciding the clustering results, an idea to develop an algorithm with this feature embedded in it was conceived. Furthermore, these algorithms perform crisp clustering which fails to capture the uncertainties in the location based dataset and this led to the development of an intelligent methodology, the first algorithm proposed in the chapter.

The proposed methodology is a first gradient based decision tree model that group location data into groups of clusters so that place or town within a cluster are highly similar and place or town in different groups are highly dissimilar. This algorithm is designed to be intelligent in the sense that it itself detects the optimum number of groups. Another main advantage of this method is that it does not restrict a place or town to one cluster as it is based on rough set theory. The location data can get expressed in two or more groups ie. overlapping of place data is possible. It clearly depicts the lower and upper approximation of the groups. Pearson's Correlation coefficient is a similarity measure that works better on continuous data. Location based data is continuous as it records the behavior of location data at many different points or conditions. So this algorithm uses Pearson's correlation coefficient as the similarity measure to find the similarity between the places and group them.

It works based on the framework of Rough sets. In the context of clustering, location based data matrix is considered as a large matrix of continuous expression values of location data under different experimental conditions. The status of the cellular process and the similarity of the places can be found by identifying the patterns hidden in the expression profile. Correlation coefficient as a similarity metric for grouping gives better outcome on continuous data like location based data (Brain *et al.* 2011).

Moreover Pearson's correlation coefficient is widely used and has been proved efficient as a similarity measure for location based data (Jiang *et al.* 2004, Anindya *et al.* 2009). So the methodology framed was designed to use Pearson's correlation coefficient as the metric for finding the similarity matrix. With the help of the similarity matrix the initial assignments to groups are done. Each object is either assigned to the upper or the lower approximation of a group. The mean of each group (lower and upper) is then taken as the centre of that place.

5.3 PHASES OF GBDT MODEL

Algorithm 1 describes the mapper and subtractor index for candidate split points. During the graph phase, the sufficient statistics contain a key (f, v), which includes the feature f and the feature value v, and the corresponding value (r), which is the weight of the current value and the model. The reducing phase combines the residuals and weights of each key. For output file, we perform a single pass in the sorted cut-offs and find the best cut globally.

This Map Reduce method reduces the problem of subtracting the number of sample values from the dimension of the number of samples to the optimal cut-off for each feature. This method specializes in datasets that have definite or Boolean features (e.g. click on data). The whole process requires another graphing task to share data for each node and one to use the current ensemble after training an entire tree. Algorithm 2 shows the pseudo-code for updating the residuals of each model.

The distributor writes samples to different outputs depending on the end of the model. The appliance code for writing in Map Reduce is trivial and skipped. The implementation of the Map Reduce implementation is relatively straight forward and requires some lines. However, since we mainly use HDFS for communication by writing multiple files when dividing a node, we suffer from high system overheads. Hadoop is currently not good for this type of algorithm.

The task of sharing data to each node and using an entire group after training an entire tree is a final one. Algorithm 2 shows the pseudo-code for updating the residuals of each model. The distributor writes samples to different outputs depending on the end of the model. The appliance code for writing in Map Reduce is trivial and skipped.

The implementation of the Map Reduce implementation is relatively straight forward and requires some lines. However, since we mainly use HDFS for communication by writing multiple fi les when dividing a node, we suffer from high system overheads. Hadoop is currently not good for this type of algorithm. Due to the high communication overhead, we shift the focus of the rest of this section to our MPI approach.

Our second approach seeks to improve communications by using MPI in Hadoop streaming rather than Map Reduce. For this implementation, we chose vertical partitioning because it reduces the communication overhead of computing a tree node. For the rest of the work, we will work with vertically partitioned data, unless otherwise noted. Load balancing was done to reduce waiting time for strollers. For our implementation, we used our own MPI Launcher for Hadoop using OpenMPI.

Algorithm 1 Aggregating candidate splits

```
map(key, value):
F ⇐ set of features
xvalue ⇐ split(value,delim)
for indexf in F do
key = (indexf, xvalue[indexf])
value = (xvalue[residual], xvalue[weight])
emit(key, value)
end for

reduce(key, values):
residual_sum ⇐0
weight_sum ⇐0
for v in values do
residual_sum ⇐residual_sum + v.residual
weight_sum ⇐weight_sum + v.weight
end for
emit(key, (residual_sum,weight_sum))
```

Algorithm 2 Partitioning a Node n

```
map(key, value):
xvalue ⇐ split(value,delim)
if xvalue[n.feature] < n.splitpoint then
residual = xvalue[residual]+ n.left_response
else
residual = xvalue[residual]+ n.right_response
end I
emit(key, value)
```

Figure 5.2 The GBDT Algorithm Model

The newly designed GBDT algorithm is a bi-clustering algorithm that performs clustering on both dimensions (rows and columns) simultaneously. The proposed GBDT algorithm was compared with existing bi-clustering algorithms like k nearest and Rough k-means (Lingras & West 2004).

All of these clustering algorithms including GBDT require the number of clusters to be specified as input. The accuracy rates of the algorithms are compared and summarized Though Rough K-means is a clustering algorithm; it is used in the comparison as it works on the framework of rough sets.

The GBDT algorithm finds out location data bi-clusters of maximum size where each location data is strongly associated with the subset of conditions.

5.4   EXPERIMENTAL   RESULTS   AND   PERFORMANCE COMPARISON OF BEST FIRST GRADIENT BOOSTED DISTRIBUTED DECISION TREE MODEL

For the experiments the user activity named as work, food, travel, park and shop is considered. The classifiers such as KNN based Classifiers, Gradient Boosted Distributed Decision Tree and best first Gradient Boosted Distributed Decision Tree are used. Table 5.1 shows the Place and Check-in Frequency for Four square categories Dataset.

Table 5.2 to 5.3 and Figure 5.1 to 5.2 shows the Prediction Accuracy for Classifiers Used and Average Prediction Accuracy across all classifiers respectively.

Table 5.1   Place and Check-in Frequency for Four square categories Dataset

Four square categories	Place frequency	Check in frequency
Work	440000	31000000
Food	620000	39500000
Travel	180000	86000000
Park	120000	13000000
Shop	380000	39000000

Table 5.2 Prediction Accuracy for Classifiers Used in Hadoop Ecosystem

Activity label	K Nearest Neighbor	Gradient Boosted Distributed Decision Tree	Best first Gradient Boosted Distributed Decision Tree
Work	73.2	75.6	77.4
Food	73.9	74.8	76.9
Travel	78.2	81.2	83.6
Park	81.4	83.4	85.7
Shop	74.3	76.5	78.2

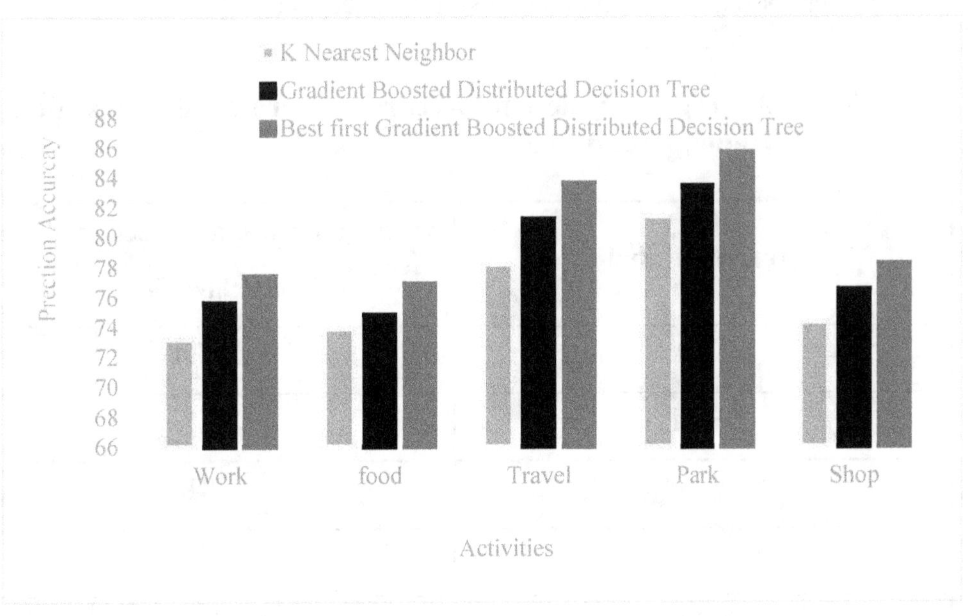

Figure 5.3 Prediction Accuracy for Classifiers Used in Hadoop Ecosystem

From Table 5.2 and Figure 5.3 it is observed that the best first gradient boosted distributed decision tree performs better prediction accuracy for the user activity work by 5.58% and by 2.35% than K-Nearest neighbor and gradient boosted distributed decision tree respectively. The best first gradient boosted distributed decision tree performs better prediction accuracy for the user activity food by 3.98% and by 2.77% than K-Nearest neighbor and gradient boosted distributed decision tree respectively. The best first gradient boosted distributed decision tree performs better prediction accuracy for the user activity travel by 6.67% and by 2.9% than K-Nearest neighbor and gradient boosted distributed decision tree respectively. The best first gradient boosted distributed decision tree performs better prediction accuracy for the user activity park by 5.15% and by 2.72% than K-Nearest neighbor and gradient boosted distributed decision tree respectively. The best first gradient boosted distributed decision tree performs better prediction accuracy for the user activity shop by 5.11% and by 2.19% than K-Nearest neighbor and gradient boosted distributed decision tree respectively.

Table 5.3   Average Prediction Accuracy across all classifiers in Hadoop Ecosystem

Activity Label	Average Prediction Accuracy across all classifiers
Work	75.4
Food	75.2
Travel	81
Park	83.5
Shop	76.3

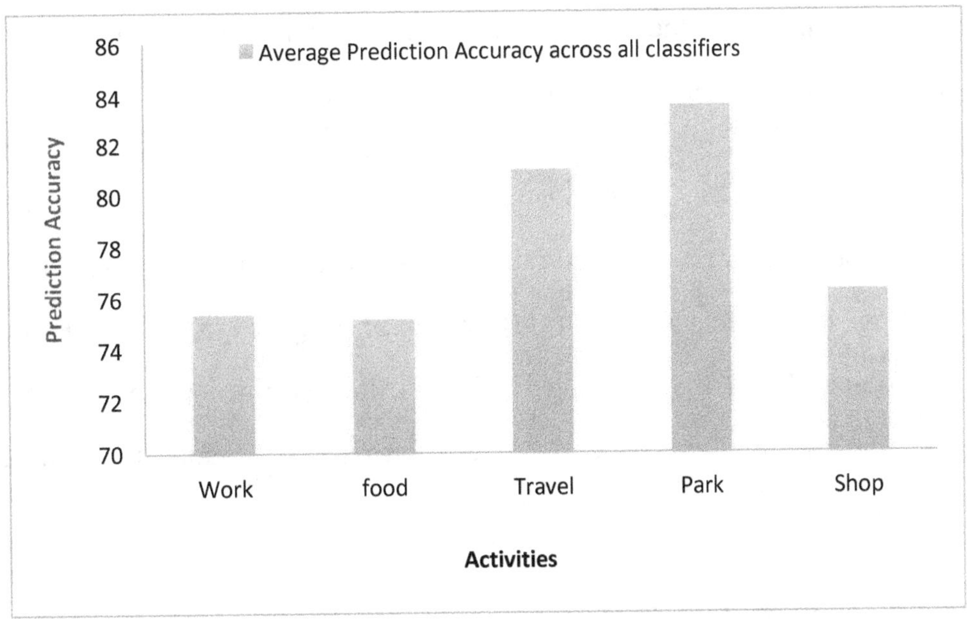

Figure 5.4 Average Prediction Accuracy across all classifiers

It is observed from Table 5.3 and Figure 5.4 that the average prediction accuracy across all classifiers for the user activity Park shows more prediction accuracy as 83.5%. Further, the proposed model and other reference methods are implemented on GPU based high performance cluster. This test bed is developed using the Hadoop and deployed in the Map Reduce program. All the proposed algorithms are implemented using the technologies such as Map Reduce. The proposed system is tested on the log entries which were collected over a period of 24 weeks.

Here, the proposed system is analyzed with the illustrative example of how it makes the recommendations to the social network user for accessing the location information. The training and prediction time of the proposed model is compared with other state of art models. Obtained results show that models built on the GPU cluster is computationally efficient than implementing the models on the Hadoop ecosystem.

The GBDT algorithm was experimented on yeast data matrix, colon data matrix and leukemia data set. The algorithm was very efficient in finding bi-clusters based on the weights assigned to the experimental conditions. From the resulting bi-clusters, the user can easily identify the location data that overlap and the location data that belong to a single bi-cluster.

5.5 SUMMARY

The proposed method is implemented in the simulation environment where parameters are included in a needed fashion. The proposed suite was experimented on different datasets and the analysis of the results proves the efficiency of the proposed algorithms. Rough clustering when applied on location based data clearly indicates the parameters that overlap.

This helps in identifying the location that plays a vital role in multiple activities. Cluster validation and comparison of the algorithms prove the efficiency of the algorithms. It has been observed that the efficiency of the algorithms vary based on the size of the data sets.

This is because, during this step, the similarity between every pair of location data is to be considered and when bi-clustering is done, it also includes the detection of condition sets. Since this step is very exhaustive, it takes much time. After the simulation execution, the simulation results are analysed based on the considered simulation parameters viz., work, food, travel, park and shop. The result shows that the proposed method effectively out performs other existing systems with respect to the considered simulation parameters. This chapter presents the design framework, functioning and results of the best first gradient boosted distributed decision tree model.

The proposed model is completely different from GBDT algorithm because it is a slope decision raised the trees bi-clustering algorithm that finds out the relationship between location data under a subset of experimental conditions. The results of GBDT algorithm demonstrate its effectiveness in finding a set of bi-clusters of maximum size with a reasonable degree of overlapping.

When compared with other algorithms, our proposed model clearly identifies location data that get abnormally expressed under specific conditions with the help of the weight matrix and also captures the uncertainties in the expression pattern of the data. Our implementation is as follows Map Reduce was run on paradigm and Hadoop. This approach required very little code and was well scaled.

However, Communication costs for reading from HDFS are very expensive, this method is useful. In fact, it was slower than the other top methods. We believe that the key factor behind the results is that our communications intensive implementation does not quite fit the Map Reduce paradigm. Our second method uses MPI and Hadoop streaming to run on the grid.

This approach has proven successful, obtained near excellent speeds, and scales with large datasets.

CHAPTER 6

CONCLUSION AND FUTURE WORK

The extract of the whole study has been clearly made concise and presented crisply in this chapter. The findings of the research work and the areas of future enhancement are also mentioned here.

6.1   CONCLUSION

The main focus of this research work is to develop novel techniques based on rough sets for clustering location data and to integrate them into a framework for the easy analysis of location based activity. The primary objective of the research work is to propose an efficient user recommendation framework which focuses on improving the performance of the classifier and recommendation engine for achieving the excellent prediction accuracy in user recommendation system. In proposed system, KNN classifier is proposed to classify the current social network user navigation to best profitable navigation profile and predict the future navigations from it. Further, the prediction accuracy is improved by incorporating the proposed framework into the recommendation engine of the user recommendation system. The aim of the proposed framework for user recommendation engine is to capture the current interest of the user in the best way and recommend only the relevant tags to the online users from the predicted links. As a result suite of clustering / bi-clustering algorithms was developed. The outcome of the research work is the Best First Gradient

Boosted Distributed Decision Tree for clustering location data. Our research work provides artistic advancement in restoration with data, innovation, location creation, KNN-based restructuring, and excellent first-time GPT travel upgrades.

The main purpose of our work is to design and implement the latest and updated recommendations with integrated system architecture. In this best first gradient boosted distributed decision tree model a new efficient method based on the KNN classifier and the GBDT algorithm is proposed for the location recommendation system. Through extensive experiments on a real dataset, the method is observed to be able to achieve good score in this recommendation scenario. In this work, we have proposed an ideal first gradient distributed decision tree model for mining heavy online user activity in LBSNs to improve the prediction accuracy.

To experiment, the user's check-in behavior and the socio-historical relationships available in the popular Foursquare dataset are considered. Consumer activities related to work, food, travel, park and shop are considered to test KNN's prediction accuracy, using the Gradient Boosted Distributed Decision Tree and the Best First Gradient Boosted Distributed Decision Tree. A novel best first tree based algorithm, is used to search location details. The new approached method is used in candidate locations for recommendation can be calculated keeping in mind the past history of users and the history of their friends. A community identification algorithm is used to identify the user's friends. The justification for deploying a first best gradient boosted tree based algorithm is that user similarity is calculated based on similarity in users' location history, which we can model well using locations. This algorithm is implemented using the Map Reduce paradigm to bring all the benefits of Hadoop environment and parallel processing.

The Hadoop ecosystem is used to implement the proposed model and other advanced models. The first gradient increased distribution decision tree estimated 5.15% for the consumer activity park and 2.72% for the K-nearest neighbour and the estimated tree, respectively. In addition, the proposed model is implemented on the GPU High Performance Cluster to achieve computational efficiency in the training and evaluation of the proposed model. A thorough analysis of the system's rating shows that it is successful and efficient to provide the most relevant travel recommendations to users at approximately 18% less response time than existing systems.

6.2   FUTURE SCOPE OF THE WORK

It is clear that the novel model produces promising and encouraging results. It can be improved and enhanced in a few dimensions to be considered as a tool. The possible ideas that can be considered for its improvement are presented here.

- The proposed model can be enhanced to include visualization techniques. Visualization of overlapping bi-clusters is an open research issue which has not been addressed here.

- Few other pre-processing methods can be included.

- The proposed clustering and bi-clustering methods can be experimented with other similarity measures.

- The efficiency of the algorithm implementation can be improved. For every retrieval of a ativity, the map reduce program takes time to access the hadoop system.

In the future, we would like to try the best XGBoost (Extreme Gradient Boosting) on the GPU platform to track prediction accuracy.

REFERENCES

1. Akdes, S & Martin, V 2011, 'DeBi: Discovering Differentially Expressed Biclusters using a Frequent Itemset Approach', Algorithms for Molecular Biology, vol. 16, no. 8.

2. Alain, BT & Ahmed, HT 2005, 'Robust Biclustering Algorithm (ROBA) for DNA Microarray Data Analysis', IEEE Workshop on Statistical Signal Processing.

3. Alberto, PM, Pedro, C, Monica, C, Francisco, T, Jose, MC & Roberto, DP 2006, 'BioNMF: A Versatile Tool for Non-negative Matrix Factorization in Biology', BMC Bioinformatics, vol.7, no.366.

4. Aristidis, L, Nikos, V & Jakob, JV 2003, 'The Global K-means Clustering Algorithm', Pattern Recognition, vol. 36, pp. 451-461.

5. Asai, M & Fukunaga, A 2017 'Tie-breaking strategies for cost-optimal best first search', Journal of Artificial Intelligence Research, vol. 58, pp. 67-121.

6. Asai, M & Fukunaga, A 2017 'Tie-breaking strategies for cost-optimal best first search', Journal of Artificial Intelligence Research, vol. 58, pp. 67-121.

7. Bakshi, S, Sa, PK, Wang, H, Barpanda, SS & Majhi, B 2018 'Fast periocular authentication in handheld devices with reduced phase intensive local pattern', Multimedia Tools and Applications, vol. 77, no. 14, pp. 17595-17623.

8. Baldi, P & Brunak, S 2001, 'Bioinformatics: The Machine Learning Approach', 2nd Edition, MIT Press.

9. Baraglia, R & Palmerini 2005, 'SUGGEST: A Web usage mining system', Proceeding of International Conference on Information Technology Coding and Computing', pp. 282-287.

10. Baraglia, R & Silversti, F 2004, 'An online recommendation system for large website', the Proceeding of IEEE/WIC/ACM Web Intelligence, pp. 199-205.

11. Barkow, S, Bleuer, S, Prelic, A, Zimmermann, P & Zitzler, E 2006, Bicat: A Biclustering Analysis Toolbox ,' Bioinformatics, vol. 22, no. 10, pp. 1282-1283.

12. Basturk. B & Karaboga. D 2008, 'On the Performance of artificial Bee Colony Algorithm'. Applied Soft Computing. vol. 8. no. 1, pp.687-697.

13. Bernard, C, Jieyue, H, Stephen, P & Yi, P 2010, 'Using Hybrid Hierarchical K-means (HHK) Clustering Algorithm for Protein Sequence Motif Super-Rule-Tree (SRT) Structure Construction , Int. J. Data Mining and Bioinformatics, vol. 4, no. 3, pp. 316-330.

14. Buluc, A, Beamer, S, Madduri, K, Asanovic, K & Patterson, D 2017, Distributed- memory breadth-first search on massive graphs, arXiv preprint arXiv:1705.04590.

15. Burke, R 2002, Hybrid Recommender Systems: Survey and Experiments', User Modeling and User Adapted Interaction, vol. 12, no. 4, pp. 331- 370.

16. Caragea, D, Silvescu, A & Honavar, V 2004, 'A framework for learning from distributed data using sufficient statistics and its application to learning decision trees', International Journal of Hybrid Intelligent Systems, vol. 1, no. 2.

17. Chen, K, Lu, R, Wong, CK, Sun, G, Heck, L & Tseng, BL 2008, 'Trada: tree based ranking function adaptation'. In CIKM. pp. 1143–1152.

18. Chen, Q, Zhang, G, Yang, X, Li, S, Li, Y & Wang, HH 2018, 'Single image shadow detection and removal based on feature fusion and multiple dictionary learning ',Multimedia Tools and Applications, vol. 77, no. 14, pp. 18601-18624.

19. Cheng, KO, Law, NF, Siu, WC & Lau, TH 2007, 'BiVisu: Software Tool for Bicluster Detection and Visualization , Bioinformatics Advance Access June 22.

20. Cheng, Y & Church, GM 2000, Biclustering of Expression Data , In Proc. ISMB, AAAI Press, pp. 93-103.

21. Chieh-Yuan, T & Chuang-Cheng, C 2010, A Novel Microarray Biclustering Algorithm , World Academy of Science, Engineering and Technology.

22. Chin, A & Zhang, D 2013 'Mobile social networking: an innovative approach'Springer Science & BusinessMedia.

23. Dayal, U, Garcia-Molina, Jacabsen, H & Yan, M 1996, 'From user access patterns to dynamic,', Comp. Networks and ISDN Sys., vol. 28, no.1, pp.1007-1014.

24. Dembele, D & Kastner, P 2003, 'Fuzzy C-means Method for Clustering Microarray Data'. Bioinformatics, vol. 19, no. 8, pp. 973-980.

25. Deshpande & Karypis, G 2004, 'Selective Markov models for predicting web page access', ACM Transaction on Internet Technology, vol.4, no. 2, pp.163-184.

26. Etminani, K, Delui, AR, Yanehsari, NR & Rouhani, M 2009,'Web Usage Mining: Discovery of the Users' Navigational Patterns Using SOM', Proceedings of First International Conference on Networked Digital Technologies, pp.224-249.

27. Floyer, D 2013, Financial comparison of big data MPP solution and data warehouse appliance'WikibonArticle.

28. Floyer, D 2013, Financial comparison of big data MPP solution and data warehouse appliance'WikibonArticle.

29. Fodor, SP, Rava, RP, Huang, XC, Pease, AC, Holmes, CP & Adams, CL 1993, 'Multiplexed Biochemical Assays with Biological Chips', Nature, vol. 364, pp. 555-556.

30. Friedman, JH 2001, 'Greedy function approximation: A gradient boosting machine'Annals of Statistics, vol. 29, pp. 1189 1232.

31. Friedman, JH 2002, 'Stochastic gradient boosting. Comput. Stat. Data Anal., vol. 38, no. 4, pp. 367–378.

32. Frigui, H & Nasraoui, O 2004, 'Unsupervised Learning of Prototypes and Attribute Weights', Pattern Recognition, vol. 37, pp. 567-581.

33. Fu, L & Medico, EF 2007, 'A Novel Fuzzy Clustering Method for the Analysis of DNA Microarray Data', BMC Bioinformatics, vol. 8, vo.3.

34. Gao, H & Liu, H 2014, 'Data analysis on location-based social networks. In Mobile social networking, Springer, New York, NY, pp. 165-194.

35. Gao, H, Barbier, G, Goolsby, R 2011, 'Harnessing the crowdsourcing power of social media for disaster relief', Intelligent Systems, IEEE, vol. 26, no. 3, pp. 10–14.

36. Gao, H, Tang, J & Liu, H 2012, 'Exploring social-historical ties on location-based social networks. In: Proceedings of the Sixth International Conference on Weblogs and Social Media.

37. Gao, H, Tang, J & Liu, H 2012, 'Exploring social-historical ties on location-based social networks', In: Proceedings of the Sixth International Conference on Weblogs and Social Media.

38. Garg, S & Jain, RC 2006, 'Variations of k-mean Algorithm: A Study for High-Dimensional Large Data Sets', Information Technology Journal, vol. 5, pp. 1132-1135.

39. Gehrke, J, Ramakrishnan, R and Ganti, V 1998, 'Rainforest - a framework for fast decision tree construction of large datasets', in VLDB, Proceedings of 24rd International Conference on Very Large Data Bases, August 24-27, 1998, New York City, New York, USA, A. Gupta, O. Shmueli, and J. Widom, Eds., Morgan Kaufmann, pp. 416 427.

40. Halkidi, M, Batistakis, Y & Vazirgiannis, M 2001 'On Clustering Validation Techniques', Journal of Intelligent Information Systems.

41. Halkidi, M, Batistakis, Y & Vazirgiannis, M 2001 'On Clustering Validation Techniques', J. Intell. Inform. Syst., vol. 17, pp. 107-145.

42. Hans-Peter, K, Peer, K & Arthur, Z 2009, 'Clustering High-Dimensional Data: A Survey on Subspace Clustering, Pattern-Based Clustering, and Correlation Clustering', ACM Transactions on Knowledge Discovery from Data, vol. 3, no. 1.

43. Hatem, M, Burns, E & Ruml, W 2018, Solving Large Problems with Heuristic Search: General-Purpose Parallel External-Memory Search Journal of Artificial Intelligence Research, vol. 62, pp. 233-268.

44. Hemalatha, M & Vivekanandan, K 2008, A Semaphore Based Multiprocessing k-Mean Algorithm for Massive Biological Data , Asian Journal of Scientific Research, vol. 1, pp. 444-450.

45. Jespersen, S, Pedersen, TB' & Thorhauge, J 2003, Evaluating the Markov Assumption for Web Usage Mining , in the Proc. of ACM WIDM, pp.82-89.

46. Jiong, Y, Haixun, W, Wei, W, Philip, Yu, Uiuc, I, Chapel, U, Hill, I & Watson, TJ 2003, 'Enhanced Biclustering on Expression Data', IEEE Symposium on BioInformatics and BioEngineering.

47. Jirong Gu, Jieming, Z & Xianwei, C 2009, An Enhancement of K-means Clustering Algorithm ,' International Conference on Business Intelligence and Financial Engineering.

48. Jun-Hao, Z, Ming-Hu, H & Jing, W 2010, 'Implementation of Rough Fuzzy K-Means Clustering Algorithm In Matlab', In Proc. of the Ninth International Conference on Machine Learning and Cybernetics.

49. Kadushin, C 2004, 'Too Much Investment in Social Capital?', Social Networks, vol. 26, no.1, pp.75–90.

50. Kruwlich, B 1997, 'Lifestyle Finder: Intelligent User Profiling Using Large–Scale Demographic Data', Artificial Intelligence Magazine, vol. 18, no. 2, pp. 37–45.

51. Lingras, P & West, C 2004, 'Interval Set Clustering of Web users with Rough K-means', J. Intell. Inform. Syst., vol. 23, pp. 5-16.

52. Lipshutz, RJ, Fodor, SPA, Gingeras, TR & Lockhart, DJ 2000, 'High Density Synthetic Oligonucleotide arrays ', Nature Genetics Supplement, vol. 21, pp. 20-24.

53. Liu, H & Setiono, R 1996, 'A Probabilistic Approach to Feature Selection a Filter Solution ,' In Proc. International Conference of Machine Learning, pp. 319 -337.

54. Liu, H & Setiono, R 1997, 'Feature Selection via Discretization of Numeric Attributes', IEEE Trans. Knowledge and Data Engineering, vol. 9, no. 4, pp. 642-645.

55. Liu, Y, Pham, TAN, Cong, G & Yuan, Q 2017 An experimental evaluation of point-of-interest' recommendation in location-based social networks Proceedings of the VLDB Endowment, vol. 10, no. 10, pp. 1010-1021.

56. Lockhart, DJ, Archana, N & Janet, AW 1996, Expression Monitoring by Hybridization to High-Density Oligonucleotide Arrays, Nature Biotechnology, vol. 14, pp. 1675-1680.

57. Luscombe, NM, Greenbaum, G & Gerstein, M 'What is Bioinformatics? A Proposed Definition and Overview of the Field', Schattauer GmbH. Method Inform Med.

58. Madeira, SC & Oliveira, AL 2004, 'Biclustering Algorithms for Biological Data Analysis: A Survey', IEEE/ACM Transactions on Computational Biology and Bioinformatics.

59. Marshall, A & Hodgson, J 1998, 'DNA Chips: an Array of Possibilities', Nat. Biotechnol., vol. 16, pp. 27-31.

60. McQueen, JB 1967, 'Some Methods for Classification and Analysis of Multivariate Observations,' In Proc. Fifth Berkeley Symp. Math. Statistics and Probability, vol. 1, pp. 281-297.

61. Middleton, SE, Shadbolt, NR & De Roure, DC 2004, 'Ontological User Profiling in Recommender Systems', ACM Transactions on Information Systems (TOIS), vol. 22, no. 1, pp. 54-88.

62. Mobasher, B & Nakagawa 2003 ,'A hybrid web personalization Model based on site connectivity', Proceeding of WebKDD, pp. 59-71.

63. Molodtsov, D 1999, 'Soft Set Theory - First Results.' Computers and Mathematics with Applications, vol. 37, pp. 19-31.

64. Narayanan, M & Cherukuri, AK 2016 'A study and analysis of recommendation systems for location-based social network (LBSN) with big data' IIMB Management Review, vol. 28, no. 1, pp. 25-30.

65. Narayanan, Murale & Aswani Kumar Cherukuri 2016, 'A study and analysis of recommendation systems for location-based social network (LBSN) with big data.

66. Nguyen, S, Nguyen, T, Skowron, A & Synak, P 1996, 'Knowledge Discovery by Rough Set Methods', In Proc. of the International Conference on Information Systems Analysis and Synthesis, pp. 26-33.

67. Nighat, N & Muhammad, AQ 2009, 'BiSim: A Simple and Efficient Biclustering Algorithm', International Conference of Soft Computing and Pattern Recognition, pp. 1-6.

68. Noulas, A, Scellato, S, Lathia, N & Mascolo, C 2012 'Mining user mobility features for next place prediction in location-based s ervices', In Data mining (ICDM).

69. Park, Y, Seo, D, Bok, K & Yoo, J 2011 'k-Nearest neighbor query processing method based on distance relation pattern. In Proceedings of the 20th ACM international conference on Information and knowledge management, pp. 2413-2416. ACM.

70. Parvesh, K & Krishan, W 2010, 'Comparative Analysis of K-mean Based Algorithms', International Journal of Computer Science and Network Security, vol. 10, no. 4.

71. Pavan, KK, Rao, AA, Rao, AVD & Sridhar, GR 2010, 'Single Pass Seed Selection Algorithm for k-Means ,' J. Comput. Sci., vol. 6, pp. 60-66.

72. Pawlak, Z 1982, Rough Sets ', International Journal of Information and Computer Sciences, vol. 11, pp.145-172.

73. Pawlak, Z, Grzymala, J, Slowinski, R & Ziarko, W 1995'Rough Sets', Communications of the ACM, pp. 88-95.

74. Priyanka Das, Asit Kumar Das, Janmenjoy Nayak, Danilo Pelusi, Weiping Ding, Group incremental adaptive clustering based on neural network and rough set theory for crime report categorization, Neurocomputing, 2019, ISSN 0925-2312 https://doi.org/10.1016/j.neucom.2019.10.109

75. Provost, F, Kolluri, V & Fayyad, U 1999. 'A survey of methods for scaling up inductive algorithms, Data Mining and Knowledge Discovery, vol. 3, pp. 131–169.

76. Ramsay, G 1998. 'DNA Chips: State of the Art ', Nature Biotechnology, vol. 16, pp. 40-44.

77. Ranjan, J & Khalil, S 2007, 'Clustering Methods for Statistical Analysis of Genome databases', Information Technology Journal, vol. 6, pp. 1217-1223.

78. Satya, RD & Satchidananda, D 2012, 'A Conspectus of Soft Data Mining in Bioinformatics', CSICommunications.

79. Scott Beamer, Aydin Buluc, KrsteAsanovic & David Patterson 2013, Distributed Memory Breadth-First Search Revisited: Enabling Bottom-Up Search , IEEE International Symposium on Parallel & Distributed Processing, Workshops and Ph.D. Forum.

80. Seo, J & Shneiderman, B 2002, 'Interactively Exploring Hierarchical Clustering Results', IEEE Computer, vol. 35, no. 7, pp. 80-86.

81. Seo, YK, Tai, MC & Jong, SB 2006, 'Fuzzy Types Clustering for Microarray Data', International Journal of Information and Mathematical Sciences, vol. 2, no.1.

82. Shamir, R, Maron-Katz, A, Tanay, A, Linhart, C & Steinfeld, I 2005, Expander- An Integrative Program Suite for Microarray Data Analysis', BMC Bioinformatics, vol. 6, no. 232, pp.1471-2105.

83. Shi, P 2009,' Clustering Fuzzy Web Transactions with Rough K Means', In Proc. of the International E-Conference on Advanced Science and Technology.

84. Sushmita, M 2006, 'Rough Fuzzy Colloborative Clustering', IEEE Transactions on Systems, Man and Cybernetics, vol. 36, no. 4.

85. Vijendra, S 2011, 'Efficient Clustering for High Dimensional Data: Subspace Based Clustering and Density Based Clustering ', Information Technology Journal.

86. Wang, H, Li, Z, Li, Y, Gupta, BB & Choi, C 2018 'Visual Saliency Guided Complex Image Retrieval' Pattern Recognition Letters.

87. Wen, YT, Fan, YY & Peng, WC 2017 'Mining of Location-Based Social Networks for Spatio-Temporal Social Influence. In: Kim J., Shim K., Cao L., Lee JG., Lin X., Moon YS. (eds) Advances in Knowledge Discovery and Data Mining. PAKDD 2017. Lecture Notes in Computer Science, vol. 10234. Springer, Cham.

88. Xiang, X, Ernst, RD, Russell, E, Zina, BM & Robert, JO 2004, 'A Hybrid Self-Organizing Maps and Particle Swarm Optimization Approach', Concurrency and Computation: Practice and Experience, Special Issue: High Performance Computational Biology, vol. 16, no. 9, pp. 895-915, 2004.

89. Xiaozhe Wang, Ajith Abraham & Kate A Smith 2005, 'Soft Computing Paradigms for Web Access Pattern Analysis ', In Proceedings of Classification and Clustering for Knowledge Discovery, pp. 233-250.

90. Yang, E, Foteinou, P, King, KR, Yarmush, ML & Androulakis, IP 2007, 'A Novel Non-Overlapping Bi-clustering Algorithm for network generation using Living Cell Array data', Bioinformatics Advance Access.

91. Yang, S, Wu, J, Du, Y, He, Y & Chen, X 2017, 'Ensemble Learning for Short-Term Traffic Prediction Based on Gradient Boosting Machine'Journal ofSensors.

92. Ye, J, Chow, JH, Chen, J & Zheng, Z 2009, Stochastic gradient boosted distributed decision trees. In Proceedings of the 18th ACM conference on Information and knowledge management, ACM, pp. 2061-2064.

93. Ye, J, Chow, JH, Chen, J & Zheng, Z 2009 'Stochastic gradient boosted distributed decision trees', In Proceedings of the 18th ACM conference on Information and Knowledge Management, pp. 2061-2064. ACM.

94. Yinghui, Y & Balaji, P 2003, 'Segmenting Customer Transactions Using a Pattern-Based Clustering Approach', IEEE International Conference on Data Mining.

95. Zhang, S, Wang, H & Huang, W 2017 'Two-stage plant species recognition by local mean clustering and Weighted sparse representation classification',Cluster computing, vol. 20, no. 2, pp. 1517-1525.

96. Zheng, Z, Chen, K, Sun, G & Zha, H 2007. A regression framework for learning ranking functions using relative relevance judgments ', Proceedings of the 30th annual international ACM SIGIR conference on Research and Development in Information Retrieval, pp. 287–294.

97. Zhou, H, Feng, B, Lv, L & Hui, Y 2007, 'A Robust Algorithm for Subspace Clustering of High-Dimensional Data', Information Technology Journal, vol. 6, pp. 255-258.

98. Zhu, W & Wang, FY 2003, 'Reduction and Axiomization of Covering Generalized Rough Sets', Information Sciences, vol. 152, pp. 217-230.

99. Zounmevo Judicael, Kimpe Dries, Ross Robert & Afsahi Ahmad 2014, Extreme-scale computing services over MPI: Experiences, observations and features proposal for next-generation message passing interface International Journal of High Performance Computing Applications, 28. 10.1177/1094342014548864.